HIGH PROTEIN 100+

HIGH PROTEIN 100+

100+ fuss-free recipes and seven weeks of protein-rich meal plans

Faye James

CONTENTS

ABOUT THE AUTHOR

Faye James is a leading voice in nutrition, wellness, and women's health, with over 20 years of experience helping individuals live more vibrant, balanced lives through the

power of food. As an Accredited Nutritionist and a member of both the Nutrition Council Australia and the Australian Menopause Society, Faye blends expert knowledge with a deeply practical, real-world approach to healthy living.

She is the bestselling author of *Everyday Easy Vegan* (2025) *The Perimenopause Plan* (2025), *The Menopause Diet* (2023), *The 10:10 Diet* (2019), and *The Long Life Plan* (2018), and now brings her signature warmth and science-backed insight to her latest title, *High Protein 100+*. This essential cookbook is a comprehensive guide to protein-rich living, designed to help readers build strength, support hormonal health, and feel energized at every stage of life.

Faye's recipes, advice, and wellness programs have supported thousands of women in boosting energy, improving digestion, balancing hormones, and feeling empowered in their food choices. Her writing has been featured in top publications including *ELLE*, *Body+Soul*, *Women's Health*, *Prevention*, *Glamour*, *Harper's Bazaar*, and *HELLO!*. She has also collaborated with major health and lifestyle brands like Woolworths, Weight Watchers, Fitness First, and Goodlife Health Clubs, providing expert insights on everything from meal planning to mindful eating.

Originally from London and now based in Sydney, Faye lives with her husband, award-winning food photographer Darrin James, and their two teenage children. Passionate about using food as medicine, she continues to dedicate her career to helping others feel their best, one nourishing meal at a time.

WELCOME TO HIGH PROTEIN 100+

For years, fat was the villain. Then carbohydrates came under fire. And now? Protein has taken centre stage, and with good reason.

We're in the midst of a nutritional reckoning. Across the board, from clinical studies to dietitian consultations to fitness circles, one macronutrient keeps rising to the top of the priority list: protein. But despite the growing awareness, most people, especially women over 40, are still not getting enough of it. The result? A wave of midlife symptoms, weight gain, energy crashes, and muscle loss that we mistakenly chalk up to "just getting older."

But what if the problem wasn't aging at all? What if the real issue was a chronic protein deficiency quietly working against your body?

As an accredited nutritionist and author who has worked with thousands of women navigating perimenopause, menopause and beyond, I've seen the transformation that happens when we begin to eat enough of the right kinds of protein. We feel fuller for longer. We gain lean muscle and shed stubborn fat. Our bones get stronger, our cravings disappear, and our moods finally stabilize.

This book, *High Protein 100+*, is a response to that growing need. With over 100 delicious, high-protein recipes, seven weeks of structured meal plans and complete shopping lists, it's designed to give you the tools to reclaim your energy, body composition and long-term health, no gimmicks, no deprivation, just balanced, evidence-backed nutrition that works.

THE SCIENCE BEHIND PROTEIN: MORE THAN MUSCLE

Protein is the building block of life, quite literally. Every single cell in your body contains it. It's essential for repairing tissue, producing enzymes and hormones, maintaining immune function and supporting every vital system, from your brain to your gut.

But it's not just about structure and function. The role of protein in appetite regulation, metabolic rate and weight management is especially significant for women in midlife and beyond. Studies show that higher-protein diets lead to greater satiety, increased thermogenesis (calorie-burning), and better body composition when compared to lower-protein plans.

Protein also plays a crucial role in maintaining muscle mass, a key factor in longevity. From the age of 30, adults can lose 3–8% of muscle mass per decade, and that rate accelerates after 60. This muscle loss (known as sarcopenia) is linked to decreased mobility, increased falls, slower metabolism and a higher risk of chronic disease.

For women in perimenopause and menopause, muscle loss can be particularly alarming. Falling estrogen levels contribute to decreased lean mass, increased abdominal fat, and a slowed metabolism. Without enough dietary protein and resistance training, it's almost impossible to preserve muscle, let alone build it.

HOW MUCH PROTEIN DO YOU REALLY NEED?

The current RDI (Recommended Daily Intake) for protein is 0.8 g per kilogram of body weight per day. But this is a bare minimum, designed to prevent deficiency, not to support optimal health, metabolic function, or body composition.

Emerging research suggests that active adults, older individuals, and especially perimenopausal and menopausal women need significantly more, ideally between **1.2 to 2.0 g per kilogram of body weight** per day. For example, a 70kg woman might need between 84 to 140 g of protein daily to preserve lean mass, stabilize blood sugar, and reduce cravings.

If she is active, for example working out 4–6 times a week, she may need as much as 2.0 g per kilogram of body weight, for example, I work out 6 days a week and weigh around 60kg so I am to get at least 120 g of protein per day.

Importantly, it's not just the total amount that matters, but how it's distributed. Studies show that spreading protein intake evenly across meals (25–35 g per meal) is far more effective at stimulating muscle protein synthesis than consuming it all at once.

This is precisely the strategy I use in *High Protein 100+*. Each day of every meal plan includes three well-balanced, high-protein meals and often one or two satisfying snacks, ensuring that you hit your target without the guesswork.

BEST SOURCES OF PROTEIN (AND WHY QUALITY MATTERS)

Let's be clear: not all protein sources are created equal.

In this book, I focus on high-quality, nutrient-dense, mostly whole food sources of protein, both animal and plant-based, including:

- **Lean meats** (chicken, turkey, beef, lamb, pork)
- **Fish and seafood** (especially oily fish, like salmon and sardines)
- **Eggs and egg whites**
- **Dairy** (Greek yoghurt, cottage cheese, kefir)
- **Legumes and pulses** (chickpeas, lentils, black beans)
- **Tofu, tempeh and edamame**
- **Nuts and seeds** (chia, flax, almonds, hemp)
- **Protein powders** (grass fed whey, pea, hemp, rice, carefully selected and used where helpful)
- Animal proteins are complete, meaning they contain all nine essential amino acids, while many plant-based proteins need to be combined to achieve the same effect. But with smart planning, both approaches can work.

The key is variety. You want a mix of complete and complementary proteins to meet your body's needs for tissue repair, hormone synthesis, and satiety. You'll also notice I've kept processed meat and low-quality protein bars to a minimum. I believe in nourishing your body, not overloading it with additives and fillers.

THE ROLE OF PROTEIN IN MENOPAUSE: A LIFELINE FOR HORMONAL HEALTH

During perimenopause and menopause, women face a trifecta of challenges: hormonal imbalance, muscle loss, and metabolic slowdown. But there's good news, protein can help address all three.

Protein provides the amino acids needed to synthesize neurotransmitters like serotonin and dopamine, which can help stabilize mood and sleep. It supports lean muscle mass, which naturally declines as estrogen drops. It also boosts thermogenesis, meaning your body burns more calories digesting and processing it than it does fats or carbs.

Multiple studies confirm that higher protein diets in menopausal women lead to better weight control, improved muscle retention, stronger bones, and even improved insulin sensitivity. That means fewer sugar crashes, more energy, and a better handle on midlife weight gain.

In this book, I've created recipes and plans with midlife women in mind. Whether you're dealing with fatigue, hot flushes, belly fat or mood swings, this is your nutritional lifeline. No more bland grilled chicken and steamed broccoli. These meals are flavorsome, satisfying, and clinically designed to support your hormones and lifestyle.

SIGNS YOU'RE NOT GETTING ENOUGH PROTEIN

Protein deficiency might sound like something that only affects people in developing nations or those on severely restrictive diets. But in reality, it's surprisingly common, particularly among women over 40, vegetarians or vegans, and those juggling busy lives where nutrition sometimes takes a back seat.

The tricky part is that signs of low protein aren't always dramatic. Often, they creep in slowly, subtle changes that we chalk up to stress, ageing, or just 'one of those things'. But these signs are your body's way of waving a red flag. It's asking for more support, more nourishment—and most importantly, more of the right kind of fuel.

Here's how your body might be telling you it's not getting enough protein:

1. You're Always Hungry... Even After Eating

Protein plays a powerful role in satiety, the feeling of fullness that keeps you from raiding the snack cupboard an hour after lunch. It slows digestion, helps balance blood sugar, and reduces the hunger hormone ghrelin, making meals more satisfying. Without adequate protein at each meal, you may find yourself constantly peckish, craving carbs or sweets, or never quite feeling full, even after a decent-sized portion.

If you've ever found yourself thinking, *I just ate, why am I still starving?*, chances are, your plate was too low in protein.

2. Your Muscles Are Weak or Wasting Away

Protein is essential for maintaining and building muscle mass. As we age, especially through perimenopause and menopause, we naturally begin to lose muscle, a condition known as sarcopenia. Without enough protein (and strength training), this process speeds up, leading to decreased strength, reduced endurance, and even changes in body shape.

If you're noticing you can't lift as much at the gym, feel weaker climbing stairs, or are losing tone despite regular activity, low protein could be to blame.

3. You Catch Every Cold Going Around

Your immune system relies on protein to produce antibodies and support immune cell function. When protein intake drops, your body's defenses can weaken, making you more susceptible to infections, viruses and longer recovery times.

If you're frequently ill, struggle to bounce back after colds, or feel constantly rundown, it might be time to assess how much protein you're really eating.

4. Your Hair, Skin and Nails Are Looking a Bit... Meh

Keratin, a structural protein, is the main building block of your hair, skin and nails. When your body doesn't get enough dietary protein, it diverts what little it does have to essential functions, like organ and immune health. The result? Dry or thinning hair, brittle nails, and dull, flaky skin.

You might not notice it all at once, but over time, these subtle beauty changes can be some of the earliest clues that your protein intake is lacking.

5. You're Losing Weight... But Not in a Good Way

If you've unintentionally lost weight and feel like you're shedding muscle rather than fat, it could be a result of protein deficiency. The body needs amino acids to repair and maintain lean tissue. Without them, it starts breaking down muscle to access the amino acids it's missing from food.

This can leave you feeling weaker, slower and less energetic, definitely not the kind of weight loss you're aiming for.

6. You're Constantly Tired and Moody

Protein plays a role in producing neurotransmitters like dopamine and serotonin, chemicals that regulate your mood, motivation and mental clarity. Without enough amino acids in your diet, your brain may struggle to keep those neurotransmitters balanced, leading to symptoms like brain fog, low mood, anxiety, or general mental fatigue.

If you're snapping at the kids for no reason or struggling to stay focused at work, don't just blame the hormones, look at your plate too.

7. You're Swollen or Puffy in Odd Places

This one may surprise you. Severe protein deficiency can result in low levels of albumin, a protein that helps maintain fluid balance in your bloodstream. Without enough of it, fluid can leak into tissues, causing swelling, particularly in the feet, ankles or lower legs.

This condition, known as oedema, is more common in extreme cases, but mild bloating or puffiness might also be an early sign of not getting enough protein to maintain proper fluid regulation.

8. You're Struggling to Heal

Protein is the raw material your body uses to repair itself. From cuts and scrapes to bruises and muscle soreness, every healing process requires amino acids. If your wounds are slow to close, your bruises take forever to fade, or your post-workout soreness lingers longer than usual, a lack of protein could be slowing the recovery process.

9. Your Hair Is Falling Out

We all lose a little hair every day. But excessive shedding or thinning, especially when it comes on suddenly, can signal a nutritional issue. When the body senses a deficiency, it prioritizes vital systems (like your heart and lungs) and temporarily shuts down less critical functions, including hair growth.

If you're pulling clumps of hair from your brush or noticing bald patches, protein intake should be one of the first things you examine.

10. You're Not Losing Weight, Despite Eating Less

It might sound counterintuitive, but if your diet is too low in protein, it can actually stall weight loss. That's because protein has a higher thermic effect than carbs or fat, meaning it takes more energy to digest and metabolize. It also helps preserve lean muscle, which in turn keeps your metabolism humming.

Without it, your metabolism can slow down, making fat loss more difficult, even if you're eating less overall.

BUT ISN'T TOO MUCH PROTEIN BAD FOR YOU?

There's a persistent myth that high-protein diets are bad for your kidneys, bones, or heart. Let's bust that.

For healthy individuals, there's no evidence that higher protein intakes within recommended ranges cause kidney damage or calcium loss. In fact, research shows that protein helps preserve bone density and muscle mass in ageing adults.

What matters more is balance. If your diet is protein-heavy but fiber-poor, low in hydration, or lacking in healthy fats, yes, you may run into problems like constipation or inflammation. That's why this book doesn't just focus on protein, it gives you well-rounded meals, rich in colorful vegetables, healthy fats, herbs, spices, and whole grains where appropriate.

High Protein 100+ isn't a meat-heavy, bacon-for-breakfast kind of cookbook. It's a smart, modern approach to fueling your body with the nutrients it needs at every stage of life.

WHAT YOU'LL FIND IN THIS BOOK

Over the next few pages, you'll discover:

- 100+ high-protein recipes: From creamy breakfasts to satisfying dinners and power snacks, all designed to be balanced and blood-sugar-friendly.
- 7 weeks of ready-made meal plans: No guesswork. Just mix, match or follow along to suit your goals.
- Complete shopping lists: For every week, every plan, because busy lives need simplicity.
- Each recipe includes a full nutritional breakdown so you can track your intake and you can personalize based on your needs, whether you're aiming to lose fat, build muscle, reduce cravings, or simply feel more energized and in control.

MEAL PLANS

WEEK 1 MEAL PLAN

DAY	BREAKFAST	LUNCH	SNACK	DINNER
Monday	Herb & Goat's Cheese Omelet	Meal-Prep Broccoli Salad with Chicken	Simple Oaty Biscuits	Indian Spiced Beef Keema
Tuesday	Mushroom & Herb Pancakes	Meal-Prep Broccoli Salad with Chicken	Greek Yogurt Protein Cake	Indian Spiced Beef Keema
Wednesday	Mushroom & Herb Pancakes	Keto Chicken & Veggie Wraps	Greek Yogurt Protein Cake	Rosemary, Salmon & Sweet Potato Tray Bake
Thursday	Berry Cottage Cheese Bowl	Rosemary, Salmon & Sweet Potato Tray Bake	Creamy Avocado & Honey Smoothie	Tuna & Caper Pasta
Friday	Egg Salad on Rice Cakes	Low-Carb Chicken Lasagna	Creamy Avocado & Honey Smoothie	Tuna & Caper Pasta
Saturday	Egg Salad on Rice Cakes	Low-Carb Chicken Lasagna	Simple Oaty Biscuits	Meal Out – Enjoy!
Sunday	Creamy Avocado & Honey Smoothie	Creamy Beef & Leek Soup	Simple Oaty Biscuits	Easy Kedgeree

SHOPPING LIST

Produce

3 avocados
1 banana
pack of blueberries
2 lemons
2 onions
2 red onions
2 shallots
1 bunch green onions (spring onions)
1 leek
2 bulbs garlic
root ginger
1 carrot
4 tomatoes
pack of mixed color cherry tomatoes
1 red capsicum
2 zucchinis
pack of chestnut mushrooms
1 head broccoli
pack of rocket (arugula)
2 sweet potatoes
coriander (cilantro)
dill
rosemary
thyme
green peas (garden peas)
mixed berries
ice cubes

Protein

boneless, skinless chicken breast
lean ground beef (beef mince)
skinless smoked haddock
salmon fillet
21 eggs
unsweetened almond milk
Greek yogurt
cottage cheese
cream cheese, reduced fat
mozzarella cheese
Parmesan cheese
Ricotta cheese
goat's cheese
hummus

Dry Goods

Basmati rice
ground almonds
oats
sliced almonds (flaked almonds)
flaxseed meal (ground flaxseed)
all-purpose flour
baking powder
vanilla extract
curry powder
paprika powder
chilli powder
red pepper flakes (chilli flakes)
garlic powder
dried oregano
ground cinnamon

Staples & Misc

honey
maple syrup
canned diced tomatoes
canned cannellini beans
canned tuna in olive oil
Dijon mustard
tomato paste
sun-dried tomatoes
jar capers
chicken stock
frozen berries
pasta shells
sea salt
rice cakes
coconut oil

SERVES 2 | PREPARATION TIME: 20 MINUTES

HERB & GOAT'S CHEESE OMELET

INGREDIENTS

2 shallots, finely diced

½ tsp dried oregano

½ tsp fresh thyme leaves

½ tsp fresh rosemary, chopped

4 large eggs, whisked

2 egg whites from large eggs

60 g (2 oz) goat's cheese

1 tsp honey

METHOD

- Add 1 tablespoon of olive oil into a non-stick skillet and sauté the shallots over low heat for 5 minutes until translucent.
- Add the herbs and cook for a further 5 minutes.
- Meanwhile, whisk the eggs and season with salt and pepper.
- Add another 1 tablespoon of oil to the pan, then pour in the eggs.
- Increase the heat to medium and sauté the eggs until they begin to set, then crumble the goat's cheese over and drizzle with honey.
- Cook until the cheese melts and the omelet browns on the bottom. Fold in half, cook for a further 2–3 minutes, then serve immediately.

Serving suggestion: Fresh bread with goat's cheese and herbs.

ENERGY 394 Cal	CARBS 10 g	PROTEIN 21 g	FAT 30 g

SERVES 2 | PREPARATION TIME: 20 MINUTES

EGG SALAD ON RICE CAKES

INGREDIENTS

6 eggs

30 g (1 oz) fresh dill, chopped

2 green onions, sliced

1 lemon, juiced

60 g (2 oz) Greek yogurt

1 tsp Dijon mustard

6 rice cakes

1 tomato, sliced

METHOD

- Boil the eggs for 7 minutes, then rinse with cold water and drain. Peel the eggs and mash in a bowl with a fork.
- Mix in the dill, green onions, lemon juice, Greek yogurt, mustard and season with salt and pepper.
- Spoon the egg salad onto the rice cakes, top with sliced tomato, garnish with extra dill, and season with pepper.

ENERGY **348** Cal | CARBS **27** g | PROTEIN **24** g | FAT **16** g

SERVES 2 | PREPARATION TIME: 30 MINUTES

MUSHROOM & HERB PANCAKES

INGREDIENTS

90 g (3 oz) mushrooms, diced

1 onion, diced

90 g (3 oz) cottage cheese

2 eggs

30 g (1 oz) ground almonds

1 tsp baking powder

90 g (3 oz) tomatoes, diced

1 green onion, sliced

4 tbsp Greek yogurt

METHOD

- Heat 1 tablespoon of olive oil in a nonstick skillet over medium heat. Sauté the mushrooms and brown onion for 5 minutes.
- In a bowl, combine the cottage cheese, eggs, ground almonds, baking powder and a pinch of salt. Fold in sautéed mushrooms, tomatoes and green onions.
- Heat another tablespoon of olive oil in the skillet. Spoon the batter into the skillet, forming pancakes, and cook for 3 minutes on each side until golden.
- Serve warm, topped with optional Greek yogurt.

ENERGY **448** Cal | CARBS **18** g | PROTEIN **22** g | FAT **32** g

SERVES 2 | PREPARATION TIME: 20 MINUTES

BERRY COTTAGE CHEESE BOWL

INGREDIENTS

30 g (1 oz) sliced almonds

400 g (14 oz) cottage cheese

200 g (7 oz) mixed frozen berries

90 g (3 oz) fresh blueberries

1 tbsp flaxseed meal

METHOD

- Toast the almonds in a dry skillet until golden.
- Blend the cottage cheese with the frozen berries until smooth and place into a bowl.
- Top the berry curd with fresh blueberries, toasted almonds, and flaxseed meal before serving.

ENERGY **377** Cal | CARBS **29** g | PROTEIN **27** g | FAT **17** g

SERVES 2 | PREPARATION TIME: 30 MINUTES

MEAL-PREP BROCCOLI SALAD WITH CHICKEN

INGREDIENTS

1 head broccoli, cut into florets

1 tsp paprika powder

1 tsp garlic powder

400 g (14 oz) boneless, skinless chicken breast

2 cloves garlic, chopped

60 g (2 oz) sun-dried tomatoes, chopped

½ tsp red pepper flakes

2 tbsp Parmesan cheese, grated

2 tbsp olive oil

salt and pepper, to taste

METHOD

- Boil the broccoli in salted water for 5 minutes until tender, drain and cool.
- In a bowl, mix 1 tablespoon of olive oil with the paprika, garlic powder, salt, and pepper.
- Brush the chicken with this marinade.
- Heat a skillet to medium high heat and cook the chicken for 4–5 minutes on each side, until golden brown, and cooked through.
- Slice the chicken and set aside.
- In the same skillet, heat another tablespoon of olive oil and sauté the garlic with the sun-dried tomatoes, salt, pepper, and red pepper flakes for 3–4 minutes.
- Toss with broccoli and Parmesan, then transfer to storage containers and top with chicken.

ENERGY **493** Cal | CARBS **30** g | PROTEIN **46** g | FAT **21** g

SERVES 2 | PREPARATION TIME: 30 MINUTES

CHICKEN & VEGGIE WRAPS

INGREDIENTS

For the wrap:

60 g (2 oz) ground almonds

1 ½ tbsp psyllium husk

¼ tsp salt

1 tsp olive oil

60 ml (2 fl. oz) warm water

almond flour, for dusting

For the filling:

155 g (5 oz) chicken breast, cooked (leftover)

60 g (2 oz) hummus

½ red capsicum (red bell pepper), sliced

30 g (1 oz) rocket (arugula)

METHOD

- In a bowl, mix ground almonds, psyllium husks, and ¼ tsp of salt.
- Add 1 tsp of olive oil and 60ml (2 fl. oz) warm tap water; mix until combined.
- Let rest for 1 minute. Knead the dough briefly and form a ball.
- Place on a surface lightly dusted with almond flour.
- Divide into 2 pieces. Roll each piece thin between parchment sheets and cut into circles using a plate as a guide.
- Cook wraps on a pan greased with ½ tsp of oil over medium heat for 2–3 minutes per side. Repeat for remaining dough.
- Spread some of the hummus on each wrap, top with the chicken, capsicum and rocket.
- Roll up and serve.

ENERGY **426** Cal	CARBS **15** g	PROTEIN **33** g	FAT **26** g

SERVES 2 | PREPARATION TIME: 20 MINUTES

CREAMY BEEF & LEEK SOUP

INGREDIENTS

200 g (7 oz) lean ground beef

1 leek, sliced

665 ml (2 ¾ cups) vegetable stock

90 g (3 oz) cream cheese

½ tsp paprika powder

1 tbsp olive oil

salt and pepper, to taste

METHOD

- Heat 1 tablespoon of olive oil in a large pot and cook the ground beef until browned.
- Add the sliced leek and sauté briefly, then pour in vegetable stock.
- Simmer for 5 minutes.
- Stir in cream cheese, season with paprika, salt and pepper.
- Cook for 5 minutes until the soup has thickened. Serve hot.

ENERGY **355** Cal | CARBS **12** g | PROTEIN **25** g | FAT **23** g

SERVES 2 | PREPARATION TIME: 30 MINUTES

LOW-CARB CHICKEN LASAGNA

INGREDIENTS

155 g (5 oz) lean ground chicken breast (minced)

2 cloves garlic, minced

155 g (5 oz) canned diced tomatoes

2 tsp oregano

2 sprigs thyme, leaves removed

1 tsp chilli powder

2 zucchinis, sliced into ribbons

125 g (4 oz) ricotta cheese

60 g (2 oz) mozzarella cheese, grated

1 tbsp olive oil

salt and pepper, to taste

METHOD

- Preheat the oven to 200°C (390°F).
- Heat 1 tablespoon of olive oil in a skillet, add the chicken, garlic, season with salt and pepper and sauté for 4–5 minutes.
- Add the canned tomatoes, oregano, thyme and chilli powder to the skillet and simmer for 10 minutes.
- In a casserole, layer the zucchini ribbons, with the ricotta, and chicken and tomato sauce.
- Top with the mozzarella cheese and place into the hot oven and bake for 25 minutes.

ENERGY 390 Cal	CARBS 16 g	PROTEIN 32 g	FAT 22 g

SERVES 4 | PREPARATION TIME: 40 MINUTES

EASY KEDGEREE

INGREDIENTS

2 tbsp curry powder

220 g (7 oz) basmati rice

500 ml (2 cups) chicken stock

315 g (10 oz) skinless smoked haddock

155 g (5 oz) frozen peas

4 large eggs, boiled

salt and pepper, to taste

METHOD

- Preheat the oven to 180°C (350°F).
- Toast the curry powder in an oven-proof pan for 1 minute.
- Add rice and chicken stock, bring to a boil, then lay the haddock on top.
- Cover the pan and place in the oven to bake for 30 minutes.
- Remove from the oven and rest briefly. Flake the haddock and stir it through the rice along with the peas and season to taste with salt and pepper.
- Serve with boiled eggs on the side.

ENERGY **350** Cal | CARBS **47** g | PROTEIN **27** g | FAT **6** g

SERVES 2 | PREPARATION TIME: 45 MINUTES

ROSEMARY, SALMON & SWEET POTATO TRAY BAKE

INGREDIENTS

2 sweet potatoes, peeled and sliced

2 red onions, cut into wedges

240 g (8 oz) canned cannellini beans, drained

4 sprigs fresh rosemary

2 cloves garlic, sliced

220 g (7 oz) salmon fillet

¼ lemon, juiced

2 tbsp olive oil

salt and pepper, to taste

METHOD

- Preheat the oven to 210°C (410°F).
- Toss the sweet potatoes, onions, beans, rosemary and garlic with 2 tablespoons of olive oil, season with salt and pepper.
- Spread on a sheet pan and bake for 12–15 minutes.
- Season the salmon with salt, pepper and lemon juice, add to the pan, and bake for a further 22–25 minutes. Serve warm.

ENERGY **511** Cal | CARBS **55** g | PROTEIN **30** g | FAT **19** g

SERVES 2 | PREPARATION TIME: 35 MINUTES

INDIAN SPICED BEEF KEEMA

INGREDIENTS

½ brown onion, roughly chopped

10 g (¼ oz) root ginger

2 cloves garlic

250 g (8¾ oz) lean ground beef

1 small carrot, diced

10 g (¼ oz) tomato paste

1 tbsp curry powder

90 g (3 oz) frozen green peas

250 g (8¾ oz) cooked basmati rice

10 g (¼ oz) fresh coriander (cilantro), chopped

2 tbsp olive oil

salt and pepper, to taste

250 ml (8.5 fl. oz) water

METHOD

- Blend the onion, ginger and garlic in a food processor until smooth.
- Heat 1 tablespoon of olive oil in a pot, add the beef, season with salt and pepper, and cook for 5 minutes until browned.
- Remove from the pot and set aside.
- Add another 1 tablespoon of oil to the pot and sauté the onion puree for 5 minutes. Now add the carrot, tomato paste and curry powder and cook for 1 minute.
- Return the beef to the pot, add 8.5 fl. oz (250 ml) of water, cover, and simmer for 20 minutes.
- Stir in the peas and cook for a further 2 minutes.
- Serve the beef with rice and garnish with coriander.

ENERGY **611** Cal | CARBS **58** g | PROTEIN **34** g | FAT **27** g

SERVES 4 | PREPARATION TIME: 15 MINUTES

TUNA & CAPER PASTA

INGREDIENTS

315 g (10 oz) pasta shells

220 g (7 oz) canned tuna in olive oil

1 tbsp olive oil (reserved from tuna can)

4 tbsp capers, drained

500 g (1 lb 2 oz) mixed-color cherry tomatoes, halved

1 tbsp dried oregano

salt and pepper, to taste

METHOD

- Cook the pasta in a large pot of salted boiling water according to package directions.
- In a skillet, heat 1 tbsp olive oil from the tuna can. Fry the capers for 1–2 minutes until crispy.
- Add the cherry tomatoes and oregano; cook briefly, then stir in the tuna.
- Toss the drained pasta with the tuna mixture, adding a splash of pasta water if needed to loosen the sauce.
- Season with salt and pepper. Sprinkle with the crispy capers and serve immediately.

ENERGY **434** Cal | CARBS **62** g | PROTEIN **24** g | FAT **10** g

SERVES 2 | PREPARATION TIME: 10 MINUTES

CREAMY AVOCADO & HONEY SMOOTHIE

INGREDIENTS

250 g (8 oz) Greek yogurt

½ tsp vanilla extract

1 ripe banana, mashed

1 ripe avocado, mashed

125 ml (4 fl. oz) almond milk

2 tbsp honey

pinch of ground cinnamon

handful of ice cubes

Optional

1 scoop protein powder

METHOD

- Place all the ingredients in a high-speed blender.
- Blend until smooth.
- Serve immediately.

ENERGY **406** Cal | CARBS **46** g | PROTEIN **15** g | FAT **18** g

SERVES 10 | PREPARATION TIME: 1 HOUR 10 MINUTES

GREEK YOGURT PROTEIN CAKE

INGREDIENTS

155 g (5 oz) Greek yogurt
155 g (5 oz) maple syrup
3 large eggs
1 tbsp olive oil
1 tsp vanilla extract
450 g (1 lb) whole wheat flour
1 tbsp baking powder
pinch of salt
pinch of ground cinnamon

METHOD

- Preheat the oven to 175°C (350°F). Grease a loaf pan.
- In a large bowl, whisk together the yogurt, olive oil, maple syrup, eggs, and vanilla extract.
- Add the flour, baking powder, salt, and cinnamon. Fold gently until just combined.
- Pour the cake batter into the loaf pan. Bake for 50–60 minutes, or until a toothpick inserted into the centre comes out clean.
- Cool the cake in the pan for 5–10 minutes. Remove from the pan and cool completely on a wire rack.

Serving suggestion: Top slices with Greek yogurt, berries, banana, and a sprinkle of cinnamon.

ENERGY **298** Cal | CARBS **39** g | PROTEIN **14** g | FAT **4** g

SERVES 12 | PREPARATION TIME: 50 MINUTES

SIMPLE OATY BISCUITS

INGREDIENTS

200 g (7 oz) oats

90 g (3 oz) ground almonds

6 tbsp maple syrup

1 tsp ground cinnamon

1 ½ tbsp coconut oil, melted

METHOD

- Place the oats in a food processor and pulse until they reach a flour-like consistency.
- Add the ground almonds, maple syrup, cinnamon, and coconut oil. Pulse again until the mixture forms a dough.
- Roll the dough into a large ball with your hands, then refrigerate for 30 minutes.
- After chilling, preheat the oven to 180°C (350°F). Lightly flour a clean work surface and line a baking tray with parchment paper.
- Roll out the dough to ¼ inch (½ cm) thickness. Use a glass or cookie cutter to cut out biscuits.
- Gather and re-roll the dough scraps until all the dough is used.
- Place the biscuits on the prepared baking tray and bake for 10–15 minutes, or until golden.

ENERGY **150** Cal | CARBS **20** g | PROTEIN **4** g | FAT **6** g

WEEK 2 MEAL PLAN

DAY	BREAKFAST	LUNCH	SNACK	DINNER
Monday	Pork, Ginger & Green Onion Patties	Rainbow Chickpea, Beet & Feta Salad	Nutty Granola Bars	Loaded Taco Sweet Potatoes
Tuesday	Pork, Ginger & Green Onion Patties	Rainbow Chickpea, Beet & Feta Salad	Nutty Granola Bars	Loaded Taco Sweet Potatoes
Wednesday	Whipped Cottage Cheese Bowl	Avocado Cottage Cheese Dip	Protein Packed Chickpea Banana Bread	Poached Salmon with Cucumber Salad
Thursday	Whipped Cottage Cheese Bowl	Oven-Baked Red Curry Chicken	Protein Packed Chickpea Banana Bread	Poached Salmon with Cucumber Salad
Friday	Carrot Mango Smoothie Bowl	Oven-Baked Red Curry Chicken	Nutty Granola Bars	Beef & Broccoli Stem Stir-Fry
Saturday	Carrot Mango Smoothie Bowl	Slow Cooker Honey Teriyaki Chicken & Rice	Ginger & Turmeric Immunity Shots	Meal Out – Enjoy!
Sunday	Zucchini Egg Nests	Slow Cooker Honey Teriyaki Chicken & Rice	Protein Packed Chickpea Banana Bread	Beef & Broccoli Stem Stir-Fry

SHOPPING LIST

Produce

2 bananas
3 lemons
2 limes
1 large avocado
box of raspberries
3 brown onions
1 red onion
2 bunches green onions (spring onions)
2 bulbs garlic
ginger root
turmeric root
mixed salad greens
2 tomatoes
2 cucumbers
1 green capsicum
1 jalapeño pepper
8 carrots
2 heads broccoli
2 zucchinis
4 medium sweet potatoes
cooked beets (beetroot)
coriander (coriander)
dill
parsley
cranberries
medjool dates
mango

Protein

boneless, skinless chicken thighs
lean ground beef
flank steak
lean ground pork
salmon fillet
tuna steak
7 eggs
milk of choice
greek yogurt
cottage cheese
feta cheese
parmesan cheese
quark

Dry Goods

Basmati rice
Jasmine rice
puffed rice
rolled oats
almond flour (ground almonds)
almonds
coconut flakes
walnuts
sesame seeds
baking powder
cornstarch (corn flour)
vanilla extract
onion powder
taco seasoning

Staples & Misc

coconut oil
honey
maple syrup
can chickpeas
beef stock
tamari
mirin
Thai red curry paste
tomato sauce
tahini
natural almond butter
natural peanut butter
spicy mayonnaise
granola
2 sachets instant espresso powder
salt and pepper

SERVES 2 | PREPARATION TIME: 15 MINUTES

ZUCCHINI EGG NESTS

INGREDIENTS

2 zucchinis

2 tbsp Parmesan cheese, grated, divided

4 large eggs

1 tbsp olive oil

salt and pepper, to taste

METHOD

- Wash the zucchinis and create spaghetti noodles using a spiralizer. Alternatively, slice into thin ribbons with a vegetable peeler.
- Heat the olive oil in a non-stick skillet over medium heat. Add the zucchini and sauté for 1 minute to soften.
- Sprinkle over 1 tbsp Parmesan cheese and season with salt and pepper. Mix thoroughly.
- Divide the zucchini mixture into four portions, shaping each into a round fritter in the skillet. Create a small well in the centre of each fritter and crack an egg into each well.
- Cover the skillet with a lid and cook for about 5 minutes, or until the egg whites are set and the yolks are still runny.
- Remove from heat, season with salt and pepper, and sprinkle with the remaining Parmesan. Serve immediately.

ENERGY 267 Cal	CARBS 7 g	PROTEIN 17 g	FAT 19 g

SERVES 4 | PREPARATION TIME: 10 MINUTES

CARROT MANGO SMOOTHIE BOWL

INGREDIENTS

500 g (16 oz) Greek yogurt, divided

220 g (7 oz) carrots, peeled and sliced

500 g (1 lb 2 oz) frozen mango

200 ml (7 fl. oz) ginger and turmeric shot (juice)

4 tbsp granola

METHOD

- Add 450 g of the Greek yogurt, the carrots, frozen mango, and ginger–turmeric shot to a blender. Blend until smooth and thick.
- Divide the smoothie evenly among four bowls.
- Top each bowl with a scoop of the remaining Greek yogurt.
- Sprinkle with granola and serve immediately.

ENERGY **313** Cal | CARBS **51** g | PROTEIN **16** g | FAT **5** g

SERVES 6 | PREPARATION TIME: 30 MINUTES

PORK, GINGER & GREEN ONION PATTIES

INGREDIENTS

900 g (2 lb) lean ground pork

4 green onions, thinly sliced

1 tsp fresh ginger, grated

1 tsp salt

1 tbsp olive oil

salt and pepper, to taste

METHOD

- In a large bowl, combine the ground pork, green onions, ginger, and salt. Mix with your hands until just combined.
- Shape the mixture into 12 patties.
- Heat the olive oil in a large skillet over medium-high heat.
- Cook the patties for 4–6 minutes on each side, or until fully cooked through.
- Serve immediately.

ENERGY 218 Cal	CARBS 1 g	PROTEIN 31 g	FAT 10 g

SERVES 2 | PREPARATION TIME: 5 MINUTES

WHIPPED COTTAGE CHEESE BOWL

INGREDIENTS

400 g (14 oz) cottage cheese

60 g (2 oz) maple syrup, divided

90 g (3 oz) fresh raspberries

30 g (1 oz) granola

1 tbsp almond butter

METHOD

- Add the cottage cheese and half of the maple syrup to a blender or food processor. Blend on high speed until smooth, scraping down the sides as needed.
- Divide the whipped cottage cheese into bowls, or containers if preparing for on-the-go.
- Top with raspberries, granola, almond butter, and drizzle with the remaining maple syrup.

ENERGY **418** Cal	CARBS **37** g	PROTEIN **27** g	FAT **18** g

SERVES 2 | PREPARATION TIME: 10 MINUTES

SESAME SEARED TUNA SALAD

INGREDIENTS

315 g (10 oz) tuna steak
2 tsp sesame seeds
60 g (2 oz) mixed salad greens
1 small carrot, julienned
1 small cucumber, thinly sliced
1 tbsp tamari
1 tbsp olive oil, divided
salt and pepper, to taste

METHOD

- Heat ½ tbsp olive oil in a non-stick skillet over medium-high heat.
- Coat the tuna with sesame seeds. Sear the tuna for 4–5 minutes, flipping halfway, until lightly browned on the outside but still pink inside.
- Divide the mixed salad greens, carrot, and cucumber evenly between serving plates.
- Slice the seared tuna thinly and place it on top of the salad.
- Drizzle with the remaining ½ tbsp olive oil and tamari. Season with salt and pepper.
- Serve immediately.

ENERGY **273** Cal | CARBS **10** g | PROTEIN **38** g | FAT **9** g

SERVES 2 | PREPARATION TIME: 5 MINUTES

AVOCADO COTTAGE CHEESE DIP

INGREDIENTS

1 large avocado

200 g (7 oz) cottage cheese

10 g (¼ oz) parsley, roughly chopped

2 green onions, roughly chopped

1 clove garlic

juice of 1 lime

¼ tsp onion powder

1 tsp milk

salt and pepper, to taste

METHOD

- Add the avocado, cottage cheese, parsley, green onions, garlic, lime juice, and onion powder to a small food processor. Pulse until smooth.
- For a silkier consistency, add the tsp of milk.
- Taste and adjust seasoning with salt and pepper.
- Serve immediately with vegetables or crackers or use as a spread on toast.

ENERGY **287** Cal | CARBS **15** g | PROTEIN **14** g | FAT **19** g

SERVES 3 | PREPARATION TIME: 10 MINUTES

RAINBOW CHICKPEA, BEET & FETA SALAD

INGREDIENTS

2 tbsp tahini

juice of ½ lemon

3 tbsp Greek yogurt

340 g (11 oz) cooked beets, sliced

155 g (5 oz) canned chickpeas, rinsed and drained

1 carrot, grated

1 green onion, finely sliced

10 g (¼ oz) fresh parsley, chopped

90 g (3 oz) feta cheese, crumbled

60 g (2 oz) walnuts, roughly chopped

1 tbsp olive oil

salt and pepper, to taste

METHOD

- Place the tahini, lemon juice, yogurt, olive oil, salt, and pepper into a small bowl. Stir to combine and set aside.
- In a large mixing bowl, combine the beets, chickpeas, carrot, green onion, and parsley. Toss to combine.
- Serve the salad topped with feta cheese and walnuts, then drizzle with the tahini dressing.

Tip: Bump up the protein by serving a baked chicken breast on the side.

ENERGY **456** Cal | CARBS **34** g | PROTEIN **17** g | FAT **28** g

SERVES 3 | PREPARATION TIME: 35 MINUTES

OVEN-BAKED RED CURRY CHICKEN

INGREDIENTS

450 g (1 lb) boneless, skinless chicken thighs

10 g (¼ oz) Thai red curry paste

60 ml (2 fl. oz) water

540 g (1 lb 3 oz) broccoli florets

2 tbsp fresh coriander, chopped, to garnish

salt and pepper, to taste

METHOD

- Preheat the oven to 190°C (375°F). Line a baking dish with baking paper.
- Place the chicken thighs in the baking dish. Mix the red curry paste with the water and pour over the chicken, ensuring it is evenly coated.
- Bake the chicken for 25 minutes, or until fully cooked and the juices run clear.
- While the chicken bakes, steam the broccoli for 3–5 minutes, until bright green and tender with a bite.
- Serve the chicken with steamed broccoli and garnish with coriander.

ENERGY 255 Cal	CARBS 13 g	PROTEIN 35 g	FAT 7 g

SERVES 8 | PREPARATION TIME: 35 MINUTES

SLOW COOKER HONEY TERIYAKI CHICKEN & RICE

INGREDIENTS

1.4 kg (3 lb) boneless, skinless chicken thighs

100 ml (3½ fl. oz) tamari sauce

90 g (3 oz) honey

60 ml (2 fl. oz) mirin

30 g (1 oz) fresh ginger, grated

15 g (½ oz) garlic, grated

480 g (1 lb 1 oz) white basmati rice, dry weight

3 tbsp cornstarch

4 tbsp cold water

2 green onions, chopped

Optional: mayonnaise

salt and pepper, to taste

METHOD

- Place the chicken thighs in the slow cooker.
- Mix the tamari, honey, mirin, ginger, and garlic, then pour over the chicken.
- Cook on HIGH for 4–5 hours, or on LOW for 5+ hours.
- Once the chicken is done, mix the cornstarch and water in a small bowl and add to the slow cooker to thicken the sauce. Let it sit uncovered for 15–20 minutes.
- Meanwhile, cook the rice according to package directions.
- Serve the chicken and sauce over the rice, topped with green onions and mayonnaise if desired.

Storage: Store leftovers in freezer-safe containers. Consume within 3 months.

Serving suggestion: spicy mayo

ENERGY **487** Cal	CARBS **65** g	PROTEIN **41** g	FAT **7** g

SERVES 4 | PREPARATION TIME: 60 MINUTES

LOADED TACO SWEET POTATOES

INGREDIENTS

4 medium sweet potatoes

450 g (1 lb) lean ground beef

1 onion, diced

3 cloves garlic, minced

2 tbsp taco seasoning

125 g (4 oz) tomato sauce

115 ml (4 fl. oz) beef stock

1 tbsp olive oil (for potatoes)

1 tbsp olive oil (for beef)

salt and pepper, to taste

For the salsa:

2 medium tomatoes, diced

60 g (2 oz) red onion, diced

1 green bell pepper (capsicum), diced

1 tsp jalapeño, chopped

fresh coriander, chopped

1 tbsp lime juice

salt and pepper, to taste

METHOD

- Preheat the oven to 200°C (400°F). Line a baking sheet with baking paper.
- Wash and dry the sweet potatoes thoroughly. Pierce them all over with a fork, rub with 1 tbsp olive oil, and place on the baking sheet. Bake for 50–60 minutes, or until tender and easily pierced with a fork.
- Meanwhile, heat 1 tbsp olive oil in a skillet over medium-high heat. Add the ground beef and cook until browned.
- Reduce heat to medium. Add the onion and garlic, and sauté until the onions are translucent.
- Stir in taco seasoning and mix well. Add the tomato sauce and beef stock. Season with salt and pepper.
- Reduce heat to low, cover, and simmer for 20–25 minutes, stirring occasionally.
- Place all the salsa ingredients into a bowl, season with salt and pepper, and stir to combine.
- Once the sweet potatoes are cooked, slice lengthwise and fill each with the taco beef. Top with salsa and serve.

Serving suggestion: lime wedges and additional coriander.

ENERGY **393** Cal | CARBS **40** g | PROTEIN **29** g | FAT **13** g

SERVES 4 | PREPARATION TIME: 30 MINUTES

POACHED SALMON WITH CUCUMBER SALAD

INGREDIENTS

2 lemons

2 cloves garlic, peeled

1 brown onion, quartered

500 g (1 lb 2 oz) salmon fillets

90 g (3 oz) Greek yogurt

1 cucumber, thinly sliced

4 green onions, sliced

30 g (1 oz) fresh dill, chopped

2 tbsp olive oil

salt and pepper, to taste

METHOD

- Wash the lemons; juice one and slice the other.
- Heat water in a pot and add the olive oil, garlic, onion quarters, lemon slices, and a pinch of salt. Bring to a boil, then reduce to a simmer for 6 minutes.
- Season the salmon fillets with salt. Gently place them in the pot and simmer, covered, for 5–6 minutes, or until the salmon is opaque and cooked through. Remove the salmon and drain.
- In a mixing bowl, combine the cucumber slices, yogurt, lemon juice, half of the green onions, and dill. Season with salt and pepper.
- Serve the poached salmon with the cucumber salad, garnished with the remaining green onions.

ENERGY 290 Cal	CARBS 10 g	PROTEIN 31 g	FAT 14 g

SERVES 4 | PREPARATION TIME: 30 MINUTES

BEEF & BROCCOLI STEM STIR-FRY

INGREDIENTS

185 g (6 oz) Jasmine rice

450 g (1 lb) flank steak, thinly sliced against the grain

1 tbsp cornstarch, divided

60 ml (2 fl. oz) tamari, divided

120 ml (4 fl. oz) beef stock

1 clove garlic, minced

1 tsp fresh ginger, grated

1 medium brown onion, sliced

185 g (6 oz) broccoli stems, julienned

2 medium carrots, peeled and julienned

2 green onions, sliced

1 tbsp olive oil

salt and pepper, to taste

METHOD

- Cook the rice according to package directions and set aside.
- In a bowl, toss the steak with half the cornstarch and half the tamari. Set aside.
- In a separate bowl, whisk together the remaining cornstarch and tamari with the beef stock, garlic, ginger, salt, and pepper until smooth.
- Heat the olive oil in a large skillet over medium-high heat. Add the steak in batches, cooking for 1–2 minutes on each side, then remove and set aside.
- Add the onion to the skillet and sauté for 3–4 minutes, until softened. Add the broccoli stems and carrots, cooking for a further 2–3 minutes.
- Return the steak to the pan, add the sauce, stir well to combine, and cook for 2–3 minutes, until the sauce thickens.
- Serve the stir-fry over the rice, garnished with green onions.

ENERGY **445** Cal | CARBS **51** g | PROTEIN **31** g | FAT **13** g

SERVES 16 | PREPARATION TIME: 45 MINUTES

PROTEIN-PACKED CHICKPEA BANANA BREAD

INGREDIENTS

220 g (7 oz) canned chickpeas, drained

185 g (6 oz) Medjool dates, pitted, divided

2 ripe bananas

3 large eggs

60 g (2 oz) almond flour

1 tsp baking powder

2 instant espresso sachets, divided

60 g (2 oz) walnuts, roughly chopped, divided

60 g (2 oz) natural peanut butter

50 ml (1.7 fl. oz) olive oil

METHOD

- Preheat the oven to 190°C (375°F). Line a baking tin with baking paper.
- Add the chickpeas, 125 g (4.4 oz) of the dates, bananas, eggs, almond flour, baking powder, 1½ espresso sachets, and the olive oil to a food processor. Blend until smooth.
- Stir in half of the chopped walnuts, pour the mixture into the tin, and smooth the surface.
- Bake in the centre of the oven for 30 minutes, or until the bread is set but still moist. Set on a wire rack to cool completely before removing from the tin.
- Soak the remaining dates in hot water for 5 minutes. Drain, reserving 4 tbsp of the soaking water.
- Using a hand blender, blend the soaked dates with the reserved date water, peanut butter, and the remaining espresso powder. Add more water if necessary for a smoother consistency.
- Spread the peanut butter paste over the top of the cooled bread. Sprinkle with the remaining chopped walnuts.

ENERGY **182** Cal | CARBS **18** g | PROTEIN **5** g | FAT **10** g

SERVES 10 | PREPARATION TIME: 45 MINUTES

NUTTY GRANOLA BARS

INGREDIENTS

90 g (3 oz) almonds, coarsely chopped

125 g (4 oz) rolled oats

30 g (½ oz) puffed rice

60 g (2 oz) dried cranberries

30 g (1 oz) coconut flakes

2 tbsp coconut oil, divided

90 g (3 oz) natural peanut butter

125 g (4 oz) honey

60 g (2 oz) quark

1 tsp vanilla extract

pinch of salt

METHOD

- Preheat the oven to 160°C (320°F). Line the base of a baking tin with baking paper.
- In a large bowl, combine the almonds, rolled oats, puffed rice, cranberries, coconut flakes, and salt.
- Melt 1 tbsp coconut oil and add it to a separate bowl along with the peanut butter and honey. Stir to combine.
- Pour the wet mixture over the dry ingredients and mix thoroughly. Spread the mixture evenly into the prepared baking tin.
- Bake for 30 minutes, or until golden brown. Set on a wire rack to cool completely for 1½ hours before slicing into bars.
- Melt the remaining coconut oil and combine with the quark and vanilla extract. Drizzle over the bars and place in the freezer for 30 minutes to set.
- Serve, or store the bars in an airtight container in the refrigerator.

ENERGY **266** Cal | CARBS **29** g | PROTEIN **6** g | FAT **14** g

SERVES 16 | PREPARATION TIME: 10 MINUTES

GINGER & TURMERIC IMMUNITY SHOTS

INGREDIENTS

155 g (5 oz) fresh turmeric root, peeled and roughly chopped

315 g (10 oz) fresh ginger root, peeled and roughly chopped

2 limes, zested and juiced

500 ml (17 fl. oz) water

METHOD

- Place the turmeric, ginger, lime juice, and water into a high-speed blender. Blend to a very fine consistency.
- Strain the blended mixture through a sieve lined with a clean tea towel. If needed, gently press the pulp with a spoon to extract more juice.
- Stir the lime zest into the strained juice.
- Pour the juice into a bottle or jar and refrigerate.

Alternative method: Use a juicer for the turmeric and ginger, then mix the juice with lime juice, lime zest, and water.

Storage: Store the juice in the refrigerator for up to 1 week. Shake well before serving.

ENERGY **44** Cal	CARBS **10** g	PROTEIN **1** g	FAT **0** g

WEEK 3 MEAL PLAN

DAY	BREAKFAST	LUNCH	SNACK	DINNER
Monday	Potato & Salmon Hash	Green coriander-Lime Chicken Salad	Dragon Fruit Power Smoothie	Cowboy Pie
Tuesday	Potato & Salmon Hash	Cowboy Pie	Superfood Oatmeal Protein Cookies	Low-Carb Shrimp Fajita Meal Prep
Wednesday	Feta Egg Bake	Low-Carb Shrimp Fajita Meal Prep	Superfood Oatmeal Protein Cookies	Broccoli Mac & Cheese
Thursday	Feta Egg Bake	Tuna Steak Niçoise Salad	Cottage Cheese Banana Bread	Broccoli Mac & Cheese
Friday	Broccoli & Cheese Quiche	Tuna Steak Niçoise Salad	Cottage Cheese Banana Bread	Ground Turkey Tacos
Saturday	Broccoli & Cheese Quiche	Ground Turkey Tacos	Dragon Fruit Power Smoothie	Meal Out – Enjoy!
Sunday	Dragon Fruit Power Smoothie	Spiced Mediterranean Fish Soup	Cottage Cheese Banana Bread	Slow Cooker Beef Bourguignon

SHOPPING LIST

Produce

5 lemons
1 lime
5 bananas
dragon fruit
2 avocados
Sebago potatoes
white potatoes
baby/mini potatoes
broccoli
bunch of green onions (spring onions)
carrots
1 cucumber
5 capsicums (3 red, 1 yellow, 1 green)
2 red onions
3 brown onions
green beans
1 head lettuce
cherry tomatoes
17 large eggs
canned wild pink salmon
tuna steaks
chicken breast
chicken sausages
lean ground turkey
casserole beef
sea bass fillet
raw prawns
cottage cheese
feta cheese
sharp Cheddar cheese
Gruyere cheese
vanilla protein powder
reduced-fat cow's milk
greek yogurt
unsweetened almond milk
cauliflower florets, frozen
cauliflower rice
parsley
fresh coriander (Cilantro)
dill
thyme sprigs
basil
chives
pitted Kalamata olives
streaky bacon
unsweetened dried cranberries
raisins
bacon

Staples & Misc

honey
maple syrup
canned whole tomatoes
canned chopped tomatoes
tomato sauce (passata)
vegetable stock
beef stock
canned white beans
Dijon mustard
tomato salsa
capers
balsamic vinegar
white wine vinegar
butter
frozen pastry
mini corn tortillas
red wine

Dry Goods

elbow macaroni
pumpkin seeds
walnuts
chia seeds
all-purpose flour
oat flour
baking powder
baking soda
vanilla extract
smoked paprika
ground cumin
ground coriander
turmeric
paprika
red pepper flakes (chilli flakes)
dried oregano
ground cinnamon
fajita seasoning
chilli powder
onion powder
garlic powder

SERVES 4 | PREPARATION TIME: 35 MINUTES

POTATO & SALMON HASH

INGREDIENTS

800 g Sebago potatoes, diced

90 g (3 oz) green onions, sliced diagonally

1 lemon, zested and cut into wedges

440 g (14 oz) canned wild pink salmon, drained

2 tbsp capers, drained

15 g (½ oz) fresh dill, roughly chopped

METHOD

- Heat 1 tbsp olive oil in a large non-stick skillet over medium heat. Add the diced potatoes, cover with a lid, and cook for 10 minutes, stirring occasionally. Add 100 ml water, cover, and cook for another 5 minutes until the potatoes are tender.
- Stir in the green onions and lemon zest. Season with salt and black pepper, and cook for 5 minutes.
- Add the salmon, breaking it into flakes, and cook for 3 minutes until heated through.
- Sprinkle with capers and dill. Serve with lemon wedges.

ENERGY 366 Cal	CARBS 37 g	PROTEIN 32 g	FAT 10 g

SERVES 6 | PREPARATION TIME: 30 MINUTES

FETA EGG BAKE

INGREDIENTS

225 g (8 oz) feta cheese block

12 large eggs

handful of fresh basil, for garnish

METHOD

- Preheat the oven to 200°C (400°F).
- Grease an 8×11-inch (20×28 cm) baking dish with 1 tbsp olive oil.
- Place the feta in the centre of the dish. Crack the eggs around the feta, then drizzle with 1 tbsp olive oil. Season with salt and black pepper.
- Bake for 18–22 minutes, until the feta melts and the egg whites set.
- Use a fork to scramble the feta and eggs together. Serve garnished with fresh basil.

Serving suggestion: Serve with wholemeal pitas or wraps.

ENERGY 278 Cal	CARBS 2 g	PROTEIN 18 g	FAT 22 g

SERVES 6 | PREPARATION TIME: 1 HOUR 30 MINUTES

BROCCOLI & CHEESE QUICHE

INGREDIENTS

315 g (10 oz) pastry

2 garlic cloves, minced

4 large eggs

240 ml milk

120 g (4 oz) shredded sharp Cheddar cheese

400 g (14 oz) broccoli florets, chopped

½ tsp oregano

METHOD

- Preheat the oven to 190°C (375°F). Press the pie crust into a 9.5-inch (24 cm) pie pan, crimp the edges, and prick the base with a fork. Freeze for 20 minutes.
- Line the crust with parchment paper and fill with weights. Bake for 12 minutes. Remove the weights and parchment and bake for another 10 minutes until the edges are lightly golden.
- In a large bowl, whisk together the eggs, milk, Cheddar cheese, garlic, oregano, ½ tsp salt, and ½ tsp black pepper. Stir in the chopped broccoli.
- Pour the mixture into the partially baked crust. Bake for 37–42 minutes until the filling is set and the crust is golden.
- Let cool slightly before serving.

ENERGY **412** Cal | CARBS **35** g | PROTEIN **14** g | FAT **24** g

SERVES 2 | PREPARATION TIME: 5 MINUTES

DRAGON FRUIT POWER SMOOTHIE

INGREDIENTS

220 g (7 oz) dragon fruit

2 bananas, frozen

60 g (2 oz) cauliflower florets, frozen

30 g (1 oz) vanilla protein powder

120 ml unsweetened almond milk

METHOD

- Combine all ingredients in a high-speed blender.
- Adjust thickness by adding more milk if needed. Serve immediately or refrigerate for up to 24 hours.

ENERGY **245** Cal | CARBS **44** g | PROTEIN **15** g | FAT **1** g

SERVES 4 | PREPARATION TIME: 35 MINUTES

SPICED MEDITERRANEAN FISH SOUP

INGREDIENTS

1½ tsp ground coriander

1 tsp ground cumin

¾ tsp turmeric

½ tsp paprika

¼ tsp red pepper flakes

680 g sea bass fillet, cut into 1.5-inch (4 cm) pieces

1 red onion, chopped

1 red capsicum, chopped

2 celery sticks, chopped

4 garlic cloves, minced

800 g (28 oz) canned whole tomatoes

370 ml vegetable stock

60 g (2 oz) fresh parsley, chopped

60 g (2 oz) fresh coriander, chopped

3 green onions, chopped

juice of 1 lemon

METHOD

- Combine coriander, cumin, turmeric, paprika, and pepper flakes in a small bowl. Season fish pieces with salt, black pepper, and 2 tsp of the spice blend.
- Heat 3 tbsp olive oil in a large pot over medium-high heat. Sauté the onion, capsicum, celery, and garlic for 5 minutes until softened. Add a pinch of salt, black pepper, and the remaining spice blend.
- Stir in the tomatoes and stock. Bring to a boil, then lower the heat to medium-low and simmer, partially covered, for 20 minutes.
- Add the fish pieces and cook for 4–5 minutes until just done. Avoid overcooking as the fish will continue to cook in the hot broth.
- Stir in the parsley, coriander, green onions, and lemon juice.

ENERGY **326** Cal | CARBS **15** g | PROTEIN **35** g | FAT **14** g

SERVES 4 | PREPARATION TIME: 35 MINUTES

LOW-CARB SHRIMP FAJITA MEAL PREP

INGREDIENTS

450 g medium-sized raw shrimp, deveined and shelled

2 tbsp fajita seasoning

1 tsp garlic, minced

1 red capsicum, sliced

1 yellow capsicum, sliced

1 green capsicum, sliced

1 medium onion, sliced

800 g (28 oz) cauliflower rice, for serving

METHOD

- In a large bowl, toss the shrimp with half of the fajita seasoning. Set aside for 15 minutes.
- Heat 1 tbsp olive oil in a large skillet over medium-high heat. Add garlic and cook for 30 seconds. Add shrimp and cook for 4–5 minutes until pink and cooked through. Remove from the skillet and set aside.
- In the same skillet, add 1 tbsp olive oil and stir-fry the onions and capsicum with the remaining fajita seasoning. Cook for 5–7 minutes, or until the veggies reach your desired tenderness.
- Divide the cooked shrimp, veggies, and cauliflower rice among 4 meal prep containers. Serve immediately or refrigerate for up to 4 days.

Serving suggestion: Avocado slices with fresh lemon wedges sprinkled with coriander leaves.

ENERGY **224** Cal | CARBS **19** g | PROTEIN **28** g | FAT **4** g

SERVES 2 | PREPARATION TIME: 35 MINUTES

TUNA STEAK NIÇOISE SALAD

INGREDIENTS

315 g (10 oz) baby potatoes, halved

4 garlic cloves, unpeeled

220 g (8 oz) green beans, trimmed

315 g (10 oz) tuna steak

2 tbsp capers

155 g (5 oz) cherry tomatoes, halved

60 g (2 oz) pitted Kalamata olives, halved

METHOD

- Preheat the oven to 175°C (350°F). Line a baking sheet with parchment paper.
- Toss the potatoes with 1 tbsp olive oil, salt, and black pepper. Place on the baking sheet with unpeeled garlic cloves. Roast for 20–25 minutes, or until the potatoes are golden and the garlic is soft.
- While the potatoes cook, bring a pot of water to a boil. Add the green beans and blanch for 2–3 minutes until tender-crisp. Transfer to a bowl of ice water to stop the cooking process. Set aside.
- Brush the tuna steaks with 1 tbsp olive oil and season with salt and black pepper. Heat a skillet over high heat, then sear the tuna for 2 minutes on each side, or until cooked to your liking.
- For the dressing, squeeze the roasted garlic from its skin and whisk it with 2 tbsp olive oil and 1 tbsp white wine vinegar.
- Arrange the roasted potatoes, green beans, cherry tomatoes, and Kalamata olives on a serving plate. Top with the seared tuna and drizzle with the garlic dressing.
- Serve immediately, dividing the salad evenly between plates.

ENERGY **419** Cal | CARBS **40** g | PROTEIN **40** g | FAT **11** g

SERVES 6 | PREPARATION TIME: 25 MINUTES

BROCCOLI MAC & CHEESE

INGREDIENTS

225 g (7 oz) elbow macaroni

345 g (11 oz) broccoli florets

2 tbsp butter

2 tbsp all-purpose flour

475 ml cow's milk

1 tsp Dijon mustard

125 g (4 oz) shredded Cheddar cheese

125 g (4 oz) shredded Gruyere cheese

METHOD

- Cook macaroni in salted boiling water until al dente. Steam broccoli in the same pot for the last 1–2 minutes. Drain.
- In a saucepan, melt butter over medium heat. Whisk in flour to make a roux and cook for 2 minutes.
- Gradually whisk in milk, add Dijon mustard, and season with salt and pepper. Simmer until thickened, about 5–7 minutes.
- Stir in cheeses until melted, then mix with macaroni and broccoli. Serve immediately.

ENERGY **407** Cal CARBS **39** g PROTEIN **20** g FAT **19** g

SERVES 6 | PREPARATION TIME: 25 MINUTES

GROUND TURKEY TACOS

INGREDIENTS

600 g lean ground turkey (minced)

125 g (4 oz) tomato sauce

1 tsp chilli powder

½ tsp ground coriander

½ tsp garlic powder

½ tsp onion powder

¼ tsp dried oregano

12 mini corn tortillas, heated

For the toppings:

6 tsp Greek yogurt

6 tsp tomato salsa

3 tbsp red onion, sliced

1 avocado, sliced

handful fresh coriander, chopped

METHOD

- Heat 1 tbsp olive oil in a medium skillet over medium-high heat. Add the ground turkey and cook for 6–8 minutes, breaking it into smaller pieces as it cooks.
- Stir in the tomato sauce, chilli powder, coriander, garlic powder, onion powder, oregano, and ½ tsp salt. Cook for 1–2 minutes to blend the flavours.
- Remove the skillet from the heat. Spoon the seasoned turkey into tortillas and add toppings. Serve immediately.

Note: 2 tacos per serving.

ENERGY **385** Cal | CARBS **35** g | PROTEIN **23** g | FAT **17** g

SERVES 4 | PREPARATION TIME: 1 HOUR

COWBOY PIE

INGREDIENTS

345 g (11 oz) chicken sausages

1 brown onion, chopped

1 tbsp barbecue seasoning

1 tsp garlic granules

½ tsp smoked paprika

400 g (14 oz) canned chopped tomatoes

200 ml (7 fl. oz) chicken stock

2 carrots, peeled and sliced

400 g (14 oz) canned white beans, drained and rinsed

4 servings Protein Boost Mashed Potatoes

60 g (2 oz) Cheddar, grated

METHOD

- Preheat the oven to 180°C (350°F). Brown sausages in a greased skillet for 5 minutes. Remove and set aside.
- In the same pan, sauté onion for 5 minutes. Add BBQ seasoning, garlic, and smoked paprika. Stir, then add tomatoes, 1 tbsp balsamic vinegar, and chicken stock.
- Slice sausages into quarters and return to the pan with carrots. Simmer for 20 minutes until sausages and carrots are cooked. Stir in mixed beans.
- Transfer the sausage mixture to a baking dish. Top with 4 servings of **Protein Boost Mashed Potatoes** (see page 107) and sprinkle with Cheddar. Bake for 20–25 minutes until golden.

ENERGY 553 Cal	CARBS 76 g	PROTEIN 33 g	FAT 13 g

SERVES 4 | PREPARATION TIME: 8 HOURS 25 MINUTES

SLOW COOKER BEEF BOURGUIGNON

INGREDIENTS

600 g (1 lb 5 oz) casserole steak, cut into large chunks

1 large onion, peeled and chopped

6 slices streaky bacon, roughly chopped

2 garlic cloves, minced

345 g (11 oz) carrots, peeled and chopped

300 ml (10 fl. oz) red wine

250 ml (8 fl. oz) beef stock

2 sprigs thyme

METHOD

- Heat ½ tbsp olive oil in a skillet over medium-high heat. Season the steak with salt and pepper, and brown for 6–8 minutes. Transfer to a slow cooker.
- In the same pan, heat another ½ tbsp olive oil. Sauté onion and bacon for 4 minutes. Add garlic and carrots, cooking for 3–4 minutes.
- Deglaze the pan with red wine, stirring to scrape up any browned bits. Stir in the stock.
- Pour the mixture over the beef in the slow cooker. Add thyme sprigs. Cover and cook on low for 8 hours, until the beef is very tender.

Serving suggestion: Serve hot with **Protein Boost Mashed Potatoes** (page 107) and cooked asparagus.

ENERGY **434** Cal | CARBS **10** g | PROTEIN **40** g | FAT **26** g

SERVES 6 | PREPARATION TIME: 30 MINUTES

PROTEIN BOOST MASHED POTATOES

INGREDIENTS

1.5 kg (3 lb 5 oz) potatoes, peeled and cubed

2 tbsp butter

220 g (7 oz) cottage cheese

2 garlic cloves, minced

60 ml (2 fl. oz) milk

fresh chives, for garnish

METHOD

- Boil potatoes in salted water until fork-tender, about 15–20 minutes. Drain.
- Blend cottage cheese in a food processor until smooth.
- Mash the potatoes with butter, cottage cheese, milk, garlic, salt, and black pepper until smooth or to your preferred texture.
- Garnish with chives and serve immediately.

Note: Use with **Cowboy Pie** (see page 103) and **Slow Cooker Beef Bourguignon** (see page 104).

ENERGY **278** Cal | CARBS **46** g | PROTEIN **10** g | FAT **6** g

SERVES 4 | PREPARATION TIME: 15 MINUTES

GREEN LIME CHICKEN SALAD

INGREDIENTS

1 head lettuce, chopped

1 cucumber, sliced

1 avocado, sliced

10 g (¼ oz) fresh coriander, torn

450 g (1 lb) chicken breast

For the yogurt dressing:

120 g (4 oz) Greek yogurt

10 g (¼ oz) fresh coriander, chopped

1 lime, juiced

¼ tsp cumin

METHOD

- Blend all dressing ingredients with an additional 4 tbsp olive oil and a pinch of salt in a blender or small food processor until smooth and creamy. Refrigerate until ready to use.
- Season chicken with salt and black pepper. Heat 1 tbsp olive oil in a pan and grill the chicken for 4 minutes per side or until cooked through. Slice into strips.
- Combine lettuce, cucumber, avocado, and coriander in a large salad bowl. Divide between serving bowls and add grilled chicken on top.
- Drizzle with the coriander yogurt dressing, toss, and serve.

Note: The grilling time for chicken may vary depending on the size of the chicken breast. Aim for an internal temperature of 74°C (165°F).

ENERGY **408** Cal | CARBS **9** g | PROTEIN **30** g | FAT **28** g

MAKES 12 | PREPARATION TIME: 25 MINUTES

SUPERFOOD OATMEAL PROTEIN COOKIES

INGREDIENTS

2 large bananas

125 g (4 oz) peanut butter

2 eggs

2 tbsp honey

2 tbsp chia seeds

1½ tsp vanilla extract

½ tsp ground cinnamon

1 tsp baking soda

90 g (3 oz) oat flour

60 g (2 oz) pumpkin seeds

30 g (1 oz) unsweetened dried cranberries

30 g (1 oz) raisins

METHOD

- Whisk mashed banana and peanut butter in a large bowl until smooth. Stir in eggs, honey, chia seeds, vanilla extract, and cinnamon.
- Sprinkle baking soda and oat flour over the mixture. Fold to combine. Stir in pumpkin seeds, cranberries, and raisins.
- Chill the dough overnight.
- Preheat the oven to 190°C (375°F). Line a baking sheet with parchment paper. Scoop 4 tbsp portions of dough onto the sheet, flattening slightly.
- Bake for 12–14 minutes until set and golden. Cool on the pan for 10 minutes, then transfer to a wire rack to finish cooling.

ENERGY **198** Cal | CARBS **20** g | PROTEIN **7** g | FAT **10** g

SERVES 12 40 MINUTES

COTTAGE CHEESE BANANA LOAF

INGREDIENTS

225 g (8 oz) bananas

185 g (6 oz) cottage cheese

1 egg

80 ml (3 fl. oz) maple syrup

1 tsp vanilla extract

1 tsp ground cinnamon

225 g (8 oz) oat flour

2 tsp baking powder

1 banana, sliced, for garnish

30 g (1 oz) walnuts, for garnish

METHOD

- Preheat the oven to 180°C (350°F). Line a 20 cm (8-inch) loaf pan with parchment paper or grease it with oil.
- In a large bowl, mash the bananas until smooth. Add the cottage cheese, egg, maple syrup, ground cinnamon, vanilla extract, and a pinch of salt. Mix thoroughly until well combined.
- Gradually stir in the oat flour and baking powder. Mix until a smooth batter forms.
- Adjust the batter consistency if needed: add a little more flour if it is too liquid, or a splash of milk if it is too dry. This will depend on the size of the bananas used.
- Pour the batter into the prepared loaf pan and spread it evenly. Garnish with sliced banana and walnuts. Bake in the preheated oven for approximately 30 minutes, or until a toothpick inserted into the centre comes out clean.
- Allow the banana bread to cool in the pan for 10 minutes, then transfer it to a wire rack to cool completely before slicing.

ENERGY **139** Cal | CARBS **24** g | PROTEIN **4** g | FAT **3** g

WEEK 4 MEAL PLAN

DAY	BREAKFAST	LUNCH	SNACK	DINNER
Monday	Tomato & Chicken Quiche	Lemon Rosemary Chicken & Couscous Salad	Blueberry Pomegranate Protein Shake	Sweet Potato Turkey Chilli
Tuesday	Tomato & Chicken Quiche	Leftover Sweet Potato Turkey Chilli	Protein Mango Fluff	Taco Beef Salad Bowl with Pico de gallo
Wednesday	Blueberry Pomegranate Protein Shake	Taco Beef Salad Bowl with Pico de gallo	Protein Mango Fluff	One-Pot Paprika, Chicken & Orzo
Thursday	Cajun-Spiced Scrambled Eggs	Tuna-Mayo Lettuce Wraps	Protein Crepes with Blueberry Sauce	One-Pot Paprika, Chicken & Orzo
Friday	Harissa Sweet Potato Fritters	Tuna-Mayo Lettuce Wraps	Blueberry Pomegranate Protein Shake	Gochujang Salmon with Garlic Spinach
Saturday	Harissa Sweet Potato Fritters	Lemon Rosemary Chicken & Couscous Salad	Protein Crepes with Blueberry Sauce	Meal Out – Enjoy!
Sunday	Protein Crepes with Blueberry Sauce	Lemon Rosemary Chicken & Couscous Salad	Blueberry Pomegranate Protein Shake	Mexican Spiced Steak with Pico de gallo

SHOPPING LIST

Produce
4–5 tomatoes
cherry tomatoes
1 red capsicum
3 onions (brown/white)
1 red onion
bunch spring onions
garlic
ginger
basil
parsley
coriander
mint
rosemary sprigs
3 limes
2 lemons
1 cucumber
1 cos lettuce
1 chilli pepper
1 avocado
1 stalk celery
sweet potatoes
blueberries
chives
frozen mango
baby spinach

Protein
ground beef
ground turkey
chicken breast
chicken thighs
smoked chicken breast
salmon fillet
ribeye steak
2 cans tuna
Greek yoghurt
sour cream
feta cheese
13 eggs

Dry Goods
shortcrust pastry
couscous
orzo (risoni)
wheat flour
all-purpose flour
sesame seeds
unsweetened cocoa powder
peanuts
1 tbsp Cajun seasoning
½ tsp dried Herbes de Provence
1 tsp dried oregano
1½ tsp smoked paprika
½ tsp ground allspice
¼ tsp ground cinnamon
½ tsp ground cumin

Staples & Misc
pomegranate juice
unsweetened almond milk
honey
coconut oil
toasted sesame oil
mayonnaise
dijon mustard
vanilla protein powder
chicken stock
black beans
sweetcorn
roasted red capsicum
black Kalamata olives
canned diced tomatoes
2 tbsp harissa
1 tbsp mirin
2 tbsp tamari
2 tbsp gochujang
vanilla extract
ginger
white wine vinegar
agave nectar

SERVES 2 | PREPARATION TIME: 15 MINUTES

CAJUN-SPICED SCRAMBLED EGGS

INGREDIENTS

6 large eggs

2 tbsp milk

2 tbsp chives, chopped, plus more for garnish

2 tbsp coriander, finely chopped

1 tbsp Cajun seasoning

1 tomato, deseeded and finely chopped

METHOD

- Whisk the eggs with milk, chives, and coriander until smooth.
- Heat ½ tbsp olive oil in a non-stick pan over medium heat.
- Add the egg mixture and cook for 3–5 minutes, stirring gently.
- When nearly set, stir in the Cajun seasoning.
- Serve the scrambled eggs with tomato, black pepper, and extra chives to garnish.

Serving suggestion: sourdough bread (not included in nutritional information).

ENERGY **266** Cal | CARBS **6** g | PROTEIN **20** g | FAT **18** g

SERVES 6 | PREPARATION TIME: 55 MINUTES

TOMATO & CHICKEN QUICHE

INGREDIENTS

120 g (4 oz) sour cream

2 large eggs

pinch of nutmeg, to taste

½ tsp dried Herbes de Provence

200 g (7 oz) cooked smoked chicken breast, chopped

320 g shortcrust pastry

90 g (3 oz) cherry tomatoes, halved

60 g (2 oz) tomatoes, sliced

10 g (1 oz) fresh basil, to garnish

METHOD

- Preheat the oven to 180°C (350°F).
- Whisk the sour cream and eggs. Season with salt, pepper, nutmeg, and Herbes de Provence, then mix in the chicken breast.
- Unroll the pastry and keep it on the parchment paper it comes with. Place the crust (with the paper) into a round baking dish or pie pan. If there's extra dough hanging over the edges, fold it in and press to make a thicker crust edge.
- Pour the sour cream mixture into the crust and top with the tomatoes.
- Bake on the bottom shelf for 45 minutes, or until golden brown and set.
- Garnish with fresh basil and serve.

ENERGY 347 Cal	CARBS 23 g	PROTEIN 21 g	FAT 19 g

SERVES 2 | PREPARATION TIME: 20 MINUTES

HARISSA SWEET POTATO FRITTERS

INGREDIENTS

205 g (7.3 oz) sweet potatoes, peeled and coarsely grated

1 white onion, thinly sliced

2 tbsp harissa

30 g (1 oz) wheat flour

white wine vinegar

5 large eggs (1 for fritters, 4 for poaching)

10 g (½ oz) fresh parsley, chopped

METHOD

- Preheat the oven to 130°C (265°F).
- Heat 1 tsp olive oil in a pan over medium heat. Fry the onion for 10 minutes until soft.
- Combine the sweet potatoes, cooked onions, harissa, flour, and 1 egg. Season with salt and pepper.
- Shape the mixture into patties (about 85 g / 3 oz each). Heat 1 tbsp olive oil in a pan over medium heat. Fry for 5–6 minutes per side until golden.
- Bring a saucepan of water to a boil. Reduce to a gentle simmer, then add 1 tbsp white wine vinegar and a pinch of salt. Create a swirl in the water, crack in an egg, and poach for 4 minutes. Remove with a slotted spoon and drain on a paper towel. Repeat with the remaining eggs.
- Plate fritters and top with poached eggs. Garnish with parsley and serve.

ENERGY **466** Cal | CARBS **39** g | PROTEIN **19** g | FAT **26** g

SERVES 1 | PREPARATION TIME: 5 MINUTES

BLUEBERRY POMEGRANATE PROTEIN SHAKE

INGREDIENTS

240 ml pomegranate juice

185 g (6 oz) Greek yogurt

30 g (1 oz) vanilla protein powder

1 tsp honey

½ tsp vanilla extract

METHOD

- Add all ingredients to a blender with a handful of ice.
- Blend until smooth.
- Pour into a glass and enjoy immediately.

Note: High in carbs to replenish energy and packed with protein for muscle repair—ideal for post-workout recovery.

ENERGY **405** Cal | CARBS **50** g | PROTEIN **40** g | FAT **5** g

SERVES 4 | PREPARATION TIME: 40 MINUTES

LEMON ROSEMARY CHICKEN

INGREDIENTS

450 g (1 lb) chicken breast
3 tbsp lemon juice
1 tsp dried oregano
1½ tsp smoked paprika
2 cloves garlic, minced
2 tbsp olive oil
5 lemon slices, for garnish
3 fresh rosemary sprigs
salt and black pepper, to taste

METHOD

- In a large zip-top bag, combine the chicken, olive oil, lemon juice, oregano, paprika, garlic, salt, and black pepper. Seal and shake to coat evenly.
- Marinate in the refrigerator for at least 1 hour (up to 8 hours).
- Preheat the oven to 200°C (400°F). Transfer the chicken to a casserole dish.
- Bake for 30 minutes, or until cooked through (meat thermometer should read 75°C / 165°F).
- Garnish with lemon slices dipped in the pan juices and rosemary.

Serving suggestion: Enjoy with Quick Feta Couscous Salad.

ENERGY **202** Cal | CARBS **2** g | PROTEIN **26** g | FAT **10** g

SERVES 4 | PREPARATION TIME: 15 MINUTES

QUICK FETA COUSCOUS SALAD

INGREDIENTS

For the Couscous:

185 g (6½ oz) dry couscous

For the Dressing:

30 ml (1 fl. oz) lemon juice

1 clove garlic, minced

4 tbsp olive oil

salt and black pepper, to taste

For the Salad:

60 g (2 oz) red onion, finely chopped

155 g (5 oz) cherry tomatoes, halved

250 g (8 oz) cucumber, chopped

15 g (½ oz) fresh parsley, chopped

7 g (¼ oz) fresh mint, chopped

60 g (2 oz) feta cheese, crumbled

METHOD

- In a medium saucepan, bring 240 ml (8 oz) water to a boil.
- Remove from heat, stir in couscous, season with salt and black pepper, cover, and let sit for 5 minutes.
- Uncover, fluff with a fork, and let cool for another 5 minutes.
- In a small bowl or mason jar, whisk together lemon juice, olive oil, garlic, and salt and black pepper.
- In a large bowl, combine couscous, red onion, cherry tomatoes, cucumber, parsley, mint, and feta. Mix well.
- Pour the dressing over the salad and toss to combine.
- Taste and adjust seasoning if needed.

ENERGY **336** Cal | CARBS **40** g | PROTEIN **8** g | FAT **16** g

SERVES 6 | PREPARATION TIME: 25 MINUTES

TACO BEEF SALAD BOWL WITH PICO DE GALLO

INGREDIENTS

For the Taco Ground Beef:

680 g (1 lb 8 oz) lean ground beef

1 white onion, diced

1 red capsicum (red bell pepper), diced

160 g (5½ oz) tinned sweetcorn, drained

3 cloves garlic, minced

3 tbsp taco seasoning

For the Salad:

255 g (9 oz) cos lettuce, chopped

1 avocado, sliced

fresh coriander, for garnish

4 servings of Pico de gallo

1 lime, cut into wedges, for garnish

1 tbsp lime juice, to drizzle

METHOD

- Heat 1 tbsp olive oil in a large pan over high heat. Add the ground beef and cook until browned. Remove and set aside.
- Reduce heat to medium-low. To the same pan, add onion, red capsicum, and sweetcorn. Cook for 5–8 minutes until the onions are soft.
- Add garlic and sauté for 30 seconds, then add taco seasoning. Season with salt and black pepper and stir well.
- Return the beef to the pan. Stir until combined and cook for another 3–4 minutes.
- In a large bowl, place romaine lettuce at the bottom. Add sliced avocado, top with a portion of the cooked ground beef, and a serving of Pico de gallo.
- Squeeze lime juice over the salad, season with salt and black pepper if needed, and garnish with fresh coriander and lime wedges.

ENERGY 343 Cal	CARBS 17 g	PROTEIN 26 g	FAT 19 g

SERVES 2 | PREPARATION TIME: 15 MINUTES

TUNA-MAYO LETTUCE WRAPS

INGREDIENTS

2 cans tuna, 140 g (5 oz) each, drained

1 stalk celery, diced

2 tbsp red onion, diced

1 tbsp parsley, chopped

1 tsp chives, chopped

4 tbsp mayonnaise

½ tbsp Dijon mustard

8–10 lettuce leaves

salt and black pepper, to taste

METHOD

- In a bowl, combine tuna, celery, red onion, parsley, chives, mayonnaise, and Dijon mustard. Season with salt and black pepper. Stir until well mixed, breaking up any large chunks of tuna.
- Serve in lettuce wraps or alongside salad.

Note: The total drained weight of tuna is 204 g (7¼ oz).

ENERGY 326 Cal	CARBS 5 g	PROTEIN 27 g	FAT 22 g

SERVES 5 | PREPARATION TIME: 40 MINUTES

SWEET POTATO TURKEY CHILLI

INGREDIENTS

1 brown onion, sliced

680 g (1 lb 8 oz) lean ground turkey

2 tbsp taco seasoning

680 g (24 oz) sweet potatoes, chopped into small pieces

3 cloves garlic, minced

480 ml (16 fl. oz) chicken stock (add more if needed)

1 can black beans, 400 g (14 oz), drained and rinsed

5 tbsp Greek yogurt, for serving

1 tbsp olive oil

salt and black pepper, to taste

METHOD

- Heat the olive oil in a large pot over medium-high heat.
- Add the onion, ground turkey, and 1 tbsp taco seasoning. Cook, adding tablespoons of water as needed to keep the turkey moist, until browned and the onions are soft. Remove and set aside.
- In the same pot, add the sweet potatoes and remaining 1 tbsp taco seasoning. Stir to coat.
- Once the sweet potatoes start to brown, add the garlic and chicken stock. Bring to a boil, then simmer for 10 minutes, or until the sweet potatoes are very soft.
- Use an immersion blender to puree the mixture to your desired consistency, leaving some sweet potato chunks if preferred.
- Return the browned turkey to the pot. Add the black beans and stir to combine. Simmer for a few minutes, adjusting seasoning if needed.
- Serve each portion with 1 tbsp Greek yogurt.

ENERGY **443** Cal | CARBS **44** g | PROTEIN **33** g | FAT **15** g

SERVES 4 | PREPARATION TIME: 55 MINUTES

ONE-POT PAPRIKA, CHICKEN & ORZO

INGREDIENTS

1 brown onion, sliced

2 garlic cloves, sliced

540 g (19 oz) chicken thigh fillets, cut into bite-sized chunks

2 tsp smoked paprika

1 can diced tomatoes, 400 g (14 oz)

500 ml (17 fl. oz) chicken stock

1 jar roasted red peppers, 200 g (7 oz), drained and sliced

80 g (3 oz) pitted black Kalamata olives

4 tbsp fresh parsley, to garnish

315 g (10 oz) orzo (risoni)

1 tbsp olive oil

salt and black pepper, to taste

METHOD

- Heat the olive oil in a large pot over low–medium heat.
- Add onion and garlic. Season with salt and black pepper. Cook for 10–12 minutes until soft and golden.
- Add chicken and cook for 3–4 minutes, stirring, until lightly browned on all sides.
- Stir in smoked paprika and cook for 1 minute. Add diced tomatoes, chicken stock, red wine vinegar, roasted red peppers, and olives. Bring to a boil, then reduce heat and simmer for 5 minutes.
- Stir in the orzo and cook, stirring regularly, for 10–12 minutes, until the orzo is tender and the chicken is fully cooked.
- Scatter over parsley leaves and serve.

ENERGY **533** Cal | CARBS **66** g | PROTEIN **38** g | FAT **13** g

SERVES 4 20 MINUTES

GOCHUJANG SALMON WITH GARLIC SPINACH

INGREDIENTS

2 tbsp gochujang

1 tbsp mirin

2 tbsp tamari, divided

1 tbsp honey

1½ tsp toasted sesame oil, divided

4 cloves garlic, grated, divided

2 tsp fresh ginger, grated

565 g (20 oz) salmon, cut into 4 portions

225 g (8 oz) baby spinach

1 tsp sesame seeds

1 green onion, sliced, for garnish

cooking spray (for baking sheet)

salt and black pepper, to taste

METHOD

- Preheat the grill to high and position a rack in the upper third of the oven. Line a baking sheet with foil and coat with cooking spray.
- In a small bowl, whisk together the gochujang, mirin, 1 tbsp tamari, honey, ½ tsp sesame oil, 1 clove grated garlic, and ginger to make the glaze.
- Pat the salmon dry and place skin-side down on the prepared baking sheet. Brush with the glaze. Grill for 5–8 minutes, depending on thickness, until just cooked through.
- Meanwhile, heat the remaining 1 tsp sesame oil in a large skillet over medium-low heat. Add the remaining 3 cloves garlic and cook, stirring, until fragrant and just starting to brown, about 3 minutes.
- Add the spinach and cook until wilted. Remove from heat and stir in the remaining 1 tbsp tamari.
- Plate the salmon over the spinach. Garnish with sesame seeds and green onion.

ENERGY **260** Cal CARBS **13** g PROTEIN **34** g FAT **8** g

SERVES 2 | PREPARATION TIME: 20 MINUTES

MEXICAN SPICED STEAK WITH PICO DE GALLO

INGREDIENTS

300 g (10½ oz) ribeye steak
2 limes, juiced
½ tsp ground cumin
½ tsp ground allspice
1 tsp dried oregano
¼ tsp ground cinnamon
2 servings of Pico de gallo
1 tbsp olive oil
salt and black pepper, to taste

METHOD

- In a small bowl, mix half of the lime juice, cumin, allspice, oregano, cinnamon, salt, and black pepper.
- Brush the steak with the marinade and let it sit while you prepare side dishes, such as Pico de gallo.
- Heat olive oil in a pan over medium heat. Cook the steaks for about 2 minutes per side, or to your preferred doneness. Season with salt and black pepper.
- Slice the steak and serve with Simple Pico de Gallo (see page 140) or your choice of sides.

ENERGY **455** Cal | CARBS **13** g | PROTEIN **31** g | FAT **31** g

SERVES 4 | PREPARATION TIME: 10 MINUTES

SIMPLE PICO DE GALLO

INGREDIENTS

300 g (10½ oz) tomatoes, finely diced

½ red onion, finely diced

20 g (¾ oz) fresh coriander, chopped

½ chilli pepper, deseeded and finely diced

1 lime, juiced

2 tbsp olive oil

salt and black pepper, to taste

METHOD

- In a bowl, mix the tomatoes, red onion, coriander, and chilli pepper.
- Add lime juice and olive oil. Season to taste with salt and black pepper. Stir well.
- Enjoy with **Mexican Spiced Steak** (see page 139) and **Taco Beef Salad Bowl** (see page 128).

Tip: Make a double batch so you have enough for both recipes.

ENERGY 87 Cal	CARBS 5 g	PROTEIN 1 g	FAT 7 g

SERVES 2 | PREPARATION TIME: 5 MINUTES

PROTEIN MANGO FLUFF

INGREDIENTS

300 ml (10 fl. oz) unsweetened almond milk

450 g (16 oz) frozen mango

90 g (3 oz) vanilla protein powder

10 g (1/3 oz) peanuts, crushed

4 g (1/8 oz) sesame seeds

handful of ice

METHOD

- In a blender, combine the almond milk, frozen mango, protein powder, and ice. Blend until smooth and creamy.
- Pour into serving bowls and garnish with crushed peanuts and sesame seeds.
- Serve immediately.

ENERGY **371** Cal | CARBS **38** g | PROTEIN **39** g | FAT **7** g

SERVES 4 | PREPARATION TIME: 30 MINUTES

PROTEIN CREPES WITH BLUEBERRY SAUCE

INGREDIENTS

125 g (4½ oz) blueberries, quartered

1 tbsp honey

125 g (4½ oz) all-purpose flour

60 g (2 oz) vanilla protein powder

2 large eggs

325 ml (11 fl. oz) unsweetened almond milk

1 tbsp coconut oil (plus extra for cooking)

1 tsp cocoa powder

METHOD

- In a small saucepan over medium heat, cook the blueberries with the honey for about 10 minutes, stirring occasionally, until they soften into a sauce-like consistency.
- In a blender or food processor, combine the flour, protein powder, eggs, and almond milk. Blend until smooth.
- Heat a nonstick skillet over high heat. Melt a little coconut oil, then pour in a ladleful of batter, swirling the pan to evenly coat the base.
- Fry for about 1 minute per side, then flip and cook for another minute. Repeat with the remaining batter, adding more coconut oil as needed.
- Spread the blueberry sauce over the crepes and roll into tubes. Dust with cocoa powder and serve.

ENERGY **229** Cal | CARBS **32** g | PROTEIN **14** g | FAT **5** g

WEEK 5 MEAL PLAN

DAY	BREAKFAST	LUNCH	SNACK	DINNER
Monday	Savoury Cottage Cheese Bowl	Chinese Chicken & Sweetcorn Salad	Protein Chocolate Chip Cookies	Chicken & Veggie Stir Fry
Tuesday	Savoury Cottage Cheese Bowl	Leftover Chicken & Veggies Stir Fry	Protein Chocolate Chip Cookies	Salmon Caesar Salad
Wednesday	Chickpea Egg Breakfast Salad	Leftover Salmon Caesar Salad	Double Chocolate Mint Smoothie	Zucchini & Beef Stir Fry
Thursday	Chickpea Egg Breakfast Salad	Mediterranean Chicken & Quinoa Bowl	Cottage Cheese Cookie Dough	Zucchini & Beef Stir Fry
Friday	Broccoli Cheese Egg Muffins	Mediterranean Chicken & Quinoa Bowl	Cottage Cheese Cookie Dough	Soy Pork Chops (with Spicy Cucumber Salad)
Saturday	Broccoli Cheese Egg Muffins	Baked Cottage Cheese Tomato Fritters	Double Chocolate Mint Smoothie	Meal Out – Enjoy!
Sunday	Korean Egg Rolls (with Spicy Cucumber Salad)	Chinese Chicken & Sweetcorn Salad	Double Chocolate Mint Smoothie	Soy Pork Chops (with Spicy Cucumber Salad)

SHOPPING LIST

Produce

cucumbers
2 red capsicums
cherry tomatoes
bunch green onions (spring onions)
1 carrot
mixed salad leaves
romaine lettuce
1 brown onion
1 red onion
1 shallot
2 zucchinis
1 lemon
baby spinach
broccoli florets
parsley
coriander (cilantro)
mint
basil
fresh ginger
bulb garlic
frozen vegetable mix

Protein

cottage cheese
18 large eggs
egg whites
Parmesan cheese
Cheddar cheese
4 wild skin-on salmon fillets
boneless, skinless chicken breasts
ground beef, lean
ground chicken (extra lean)
pork chops
Greek yogurt (full-fat)
sliced ham
3 anchovy fillets

Dry Goods

spelt flour
almond flour
vanilla protein powder
chocolate protein powder
cocoa powder
dark chocolate chips
coconut sugar
cornstarch
dried oregano
dried Herbes de Provence
red chilli flakes
paprika
sesame seeds
walnuts
pistachios
cacao nibs

Staples & Misc

480 g (16.9 oz) canned chickpeas
400 g (14 oz) canned sweet corn
1L (36 oz) chicken broth
sun-dried tomatoes in oil
chocolate almond milk
gochujang paste (korean red chilli paste)
maple syrup
balsamic vinegar
honey
tamari
rice vinegar
toasted sesame oil
mayonnaise
vanilla extract

SERVES 1 | PREPARATION TIME: 5 MINUTES

Savory Cottage Cheese Bowl

INGREDIENTS

185 g (7 oz) low-fat cottage cheese

1 tbsp chives, chopped

¼ cucumber, sliced

¼ capsicum (red bell pepper), seeded and chopped

5 cherry tomatoes, halved

1 tbsp pistachios, chopped

salt and black pepper, to taste

METHOD

- In a small bowl, mix the cottage cheese with chives and season with salt and black pepper.
- Layer the cucumber, capsicum, and tomatoes on top.
- Garnish with pistachios.
- Sprinkle with additional black pepper, if desired.

ENERGY **276** Cal | CARBS **17** g | PROTEIN **25** g | FAT **12** g

SERVES 4 | PREPARATION TIME: 17 MINUTES

KOREAN EGG ROLLS

INGREDIENTS

5 large eggs

¼ tsp sugar

2 tbsp green onions, chopped

2 tbsp carrots, shredded

2 tbsp ham, chopped

4 servings of Spicy Cucumber Salad

salt, to taste

METHOD

- In a bowl, beat the eggs with 2 tbsp water, salt, and sugar. Stir in the green onions, carrots, and ham.
- Heat a 10-inch (25 cm) skillet over medium-low heat and lightly coat with oil.
- Pour about 120 ml (4 oz) of the egg mixture into the pan, swirl to distribute evenly, and cook for 2–3 minutes until the edges set.
- Lower the heat. Once the centre is no longer runny, roll one edge of the egg sheet toward the centre, stopping just before the end.
- Move the roll to one side of the pan. Lightly coat the empty side with oil.
- Pour another 120 ml (4 oz) of egg mixture, starting where the roll ends. Cook until set, then roll again.
- Repeat until all the egg mixture is used.
- Raise the heat to medium and cook the roll on all sides until golden.
- Transfer to a board, let cool for 2 minutes, then slice into 2 cm (¾-inch) pieces.
- Serve warm or at room temperature with **Spicy Cucumber Salad** (see page 171).

ENERGY **253** Cal | CARBS **13** g | PROTEIN **12** g | Fat **17** g

SERVES 4 | PREPARATION TIME: 5 MINUTES

CHICKPEA EGG BREAKFAST SALAD

INGREDIENTS

480 g (17 oz) canned chickpeas, drained and rinsed

6 large, hard-boiled eggs, sliced

2 tbsp red onion, chopped

1 tbsp parsley, chopped

2 tbsp olive oil

2 tbsp apple cider vinegar

salt and black pepper, to taste

METHOD

- Combine chickpeas, eggs, and red onion in a medium bowl.
- Drizzle with olive oil and apple cider vinegar, then toss to coat.
- Stir in parsley and season with salt and black pepper.
- Serve immediately or refrigerate for up to 5 days.

ENERGY **369** Cal | CARBS **34** g | PROTEIN **20** g | FAT **17** g

MAKES 8 | PREPARATION TIME: 35 MINUTES

BROCCOLI CHEESE EGG MUFFINS

INGREDIENTS

340 g (12 oz) broccoli florets

4 large eggs

240 ml (8 fl. oz) egg whites

30 g (1 oz) Parmesan cheese, grated

30 g (1 oz) Cheddar cheese, shredded

2 tsp olive oil

salt and black pepper, to taste

METHOD

- Preheat the oven to 175°C (350°F). Steam the broccoli for 3–5 minutes until tender.
- Crumble into smaller pieces, drizzle with 1 tsp olive oil, and season with salt and black pepper.
- Spray a muffin tin with the remaining 1 tsp olive oil. Divide the broccoli among 8 cups.
- Beat the eggs and egg whites, stir in Parmesan, salt, and black pepper. Pour over the broccoli, filling cups ¾ full.
- Sprinkle Cheddar on top.
- Bake for 20 minutes until set and golden.
- Serve immediately or cool and wrap for storage.

Note: 2 muffins = 1 serving.

ENERGY **203** Cal | CARBS **7** g | PROTEIN **19** g | FAT **11** g

SERVES 2 | PREPARATION TIME: 30 MINUTES

MEDITERRANEAN CHICKEN & QUINOA BOWL

INGREDIENTS

125 g (4 oz) quinoa

60 g (2 oz) sun-dried tomatoes in oil

1 clove garlic, peeled

1 tsp dried oregano

½ tsp paprika powder

240 g (8½ oz) boneless, skinless chicken breast

1 red capsicum, diced

60 g (2 oz) baby spinach

220 g (8 oz) cherry tomatoes, halved

2 tbsp olive oil

salt and black pepper, to taste

METHOD

- Cook quinoa according to package instructions, then set aside.
- Blend sun-dried tomatoes, garlic, oregano, 1 tbsp olive oil, paprika, salt, and black pepper into a marinade.
- Rub chicken with marinade and let sit for 10 minutes.
- Heat a grill pan over medium heat and cook chicken 7–8 minutes per side until cooked through.
- Add capsicum, spinach, and tomatoes to the pan, season, and cook for 5 minutes.
- Mix quinoa with veggies. Slice chicken and serve on top, drizzling with the remaining olive oil if desired.

ENERGY **606** Cal	CARBS **61** g	PROTEIN **41** g	Fat **22** g

SERVES 2 | PREPARATION TIME: 30 MINUTES

BAKED COTTAGE CHEESE TOMATO FRITTERS

INGREDIENTS

400 g (14 oz) cottage cheese

60 g (2 oz) sun-dried tomatoes in oil, finely chopped

2 cloves garlic, peeled and crushed

2 green onions, sliced

6 g (¼ oz) fresh basil, sliced

1 medium egg

1 tsp dried Herbes de Provence

155 g (5½ oz) spelt flour

90 g (3 oz) mixed greens

160 g (5½ oz) cherry tomatoes, halved

1 tbsp balsamic vinegar

1 tbsp olive oil

salt and black pepper, to taste

METHOD

- Preheat the oven to 210°C (410°F).
- Mix cottage cheese, sun-dried tomatoes, garlic, green onions, basil, egg, Herbes de Provence, salt, and black pepper. Stir in spelt flour.
- Line a baking sheet and spoon 2 tbsp portions onto it.
- Bake for 15–20 minutes until golden.
- Toss greens and tomatoes with olive oil and balsamic vinegar, season, and serve with fritters.

ENERGY **346** Cal | CARBS **42** g | PROTEIN **22** g | FAT **10** g

SERVES 2 | PREPARATION TIME: 35 MINUTES

ZUCCHINI & BEEF STIR FRY

INGREDIENTS

300 g (10½ oz) ground beef
1 brown onion, diced
2 zucchinis, sliced
125 g (4 oz) cheese, grated
½ tsp sweet paprika
1 tbsp olive oil
salt and black pepper, to taste

METHOD

- Heat olive oil in a pan over medium heat. Sauté onion and beef for 5 minutes, seasoning with paprika, salt, and black pepper.
- Add zucchini, cover, and simmer on low for 15 minutes until tender.
- Stir in cheese and let it melt. Serve hot.

ENERGY **309** Cal | CARBS **7** g | PROTEIN **23** g | FAT **21** g

SERVES 4 | PREPARATION TIME: 30 MINUTES

SALMON CAESAR SALAD

INGREDIENTS

1 lemon, halved

1 clove garlic, minced

30 g (1 oz) Parmesan cheese, grated

60 g (2 oz) mayonnaise

3 anchovy fillets, minced

250 g (8 oz) Romaine lettuce, torn

4 wild skin-on salmon fillets

salt and black pepper, to taste

METHOD

- Squeeze half the lemon to extract 15 ml (1 tbsp) of juice. Add the juice to a large bowl with the garlic, anchovy fillets, Parmesan cheese, and mayonnaise. Stir and set aside.
- Season the salmon with salt and black pepper.
- Heat 1 tbsp olive oil in a large skillet over medium-high heat. Place the salmon skin-side down, cover, and cook for 5 minutes until the skin browns. Flip and cook for 2 more minutes or until the salmon is cooked through.
- Squeeze the remaining lemon juice over the salmon. Add the Romaine lettuce to the bowl with the dressing and toss until well coated.
- Divide the salad between plates and top each with salmon.

ENERGY **417** Cal | CARBS **5** g | PROTEIN **43** g | FAT **25** g

SERVES 4 | PREPARATION TIME: 25 MINUTES

CHINESE CHICKEN & SWEETCORN SOUP

INGREDIENTS

400 g (14 oz) chicken breast

1 lt. (4 cups) chicken stock

400 g (14 oz) canned sweetcorn

3 tbsp cornstarch

2 large eggs, beaten

1 tsp sesame oil

chives, chopped, for garnish

salt and black pepper, to taste

METHOD

- In a large pot, bring the chicken stock to a simmer. Add the chicken breast, cover, and poach over low heat for 10–12 minutes until fully cooked. Remove, let cool slightly, then shred. Skim off any foam from the broth.
- Increase the heat to medium and bring the broth back to a simmer. Add the sweetcorn and stir.
- In a small bowl, mix the cornstarch with 5 tbsp water to make a slurry. Gradually stir it into the soup and let it simmer for 1 minute until thickened. Season with salt and black pepper.
- Slowly pour in the beaten eggs, stirring to create egg ribbons.
- Add the shredded chicken back to the pot and cook for 1 more minute.
- Finish with sesame oil and a dash of pepper. Garnish with chopped chives and serve.

ENERGY **292** Cal	CARBS **25** g	PROTEIN **30** g	FAT **8** g

SERVES 2 | PREPARATION TIME: 30 MINUTES

CHICKEN & VEGGIE STIR FRY

INGREDIENTS

½ red onion, sliced

2 cloves garlic, minced

340 g (12 oz) ground chicken, extra lean

250 g (9 oz) frozen vegetable mix

1 tbsp honey

2 tbsp tamari

1 tbsp coriander, chopped

salt and black pepper, to taste

METHOD

- Heat a nonstick pan over medium heat. Add the onion and a splash of water, stir, and cook for 5 minutes, until soft.
- Add garlic and cook for 1–2 minutes.
- Add chicken and cook for 5 minutes, breaking it up as it browns.
- Stir in the vegetable mix and cook for 15–17 minutes until tender.
- Add honey and tamari, stir, and season with salt and black pepper.
- Top with coriander, divide between plates, and enjoy.

ENERGY **390** Cal	CARBS **30** g	PROTEIN **36** g	FAT **14** g

SERVES 2 | PREPARATION TIME: 20 MINUTES

SOY PORK CHOPS

INGREDIENTS

340 g (12 oz) pork chops

20 g (¾ oz) ginger, peeled and finely diced

2 cloves garlic, minced

5 tbsp tamari

3 tbsp honey

½ tsp sesame oil

2 tsp rice vinegar

2 green onions, thinly sliced

salt and black pepper, to taste

2 servings of Spicy Cucumber Salad

METHOD

- In a small bowl, mix ginger, garlic, tamari, honey, 1 tbsp water, sesame oil, and rice vinegar. Set aside.
- Heat 1 tbsp olive oil in a skillet over medium-high heat. Pat the pork chops dry and season with salt and black pepper.
- Sear the pork chops for 3 minutes per side until browned. Remove them from the pan and reduce the heat to medium.
- Pour in the soy glaze mixture and cook for 1 minute, stirring until slightly thickened.
- Return pork chops to the pan and coat in the glaze. Remove from heat.
- Garnish with sliced green onions and serve with **Spicy Cucumber Salad** (see page 171).

ENERGY **610** Cal | CARBS **42** g | PROTEIN **43** g | FAT **30** g

SERVES 4 | PREPARATION TIME: 55 MINUTES

SPICY CUCUMBER SALAD

INGREDIENTS

680 g cucumbers

1 large shallot, thinly sliced

2 green onions, sliced (dark green pieces left for garnish)

1 tbsp white sesame seeds, toasted

1 tsp salt

For the Dressing:

2 tbsp gochujang (Korean red chilli paste)

½ tbsp red chilli flakes

1½ tbsp toasted sesame oil

1 tbsp tamari

1 tbsp rice vinegar

2 tsp (8 g) agave nectar or organic cane sugar

3 cloves garlic, minced or crushed

METHOD

- Slice off the ends of the cucumbers, then cut them in half lengthwise. Smash each piece with the flat side of a knife until it cracks, then tear it into bite-sized chunks.
- Place the cucumbers in a colander over a bowl. Sprinkle with salt and toss. Let it rest in the fridge for 30 minutes (or up to 4 hours).
- To make the dressing, whisk together gochujang, red chilli flakes, sesame oil, tamari, rice vinegar, sugar, and garlic in a large bowl.
- After resting, discard excess water from the cucumbers. Squeeze a handful at a time to remove extra moisture.
- Add cucumbers, shallots, and green onion whites to the dressing. Massage with your hands for 1 minute to coat.
- Before serving, sprinkle with sesame seeds and green onion greens.

ENERGY **119** Cal | CARBS **11** g | PROTEIN **3** g | FAT **7** g

SERVES 8 | PREPARATION TIME: 5 MINUTES

COTTAGE CHEESE COOKIE DOUGH

INGREDIENTS

250 g (8 oz) cottage cheese

1 tsp vanilla extract

2 tbsp maple syrup

60 g (2 oz) almond flour

30 g (1 oz) vanilla protein powder

90 g (3 oz) chocolate chunks

salt, a pinch

METHOD

- In a blender, combine cottage cheese, vanilla extract, maple syrup, and a pinch of salt. Blend until smooth.
- Transfer to a bowl and mix in almond flour and protein powder until well combined.
- Fold in chocolate chunks and enjoy.

ENERGY **336** Cal | CARBS **22** g | PROTEIN **17** g | FAT **20** g

SERVES 1 | PREPARATION TIME: 5 MINUTES

DOUBLE CHOCOLATE MINT SMOOTHIE

INGREDIENTS

30 g (1 oz) chocolate protein powder

180 ml (6 fl. oz) chocolate almond milk

1 tbsp walnuts

2 tbsp unsweetened cocoa powder

1 tbsp cacao nibs

2 fresh mint leaves

METHOD

- Add all ingredients to a blender in the listed order.
- Add 4 ice cubes and 4 tbsp (60 ml) water, then blend until smooth.
- Serve immediately.

ENERGY **264** Cal	CARBS **11** g	PROTEIN **28** g	FAT **12** g

MAKES 9 COOKIES | PREPARATION TIME: 15 MINUTES

PROTEIN CHOCOLATE CHIP COOKIES

INGREDIENTS

225 g (7 oz) Greek yogurt

1 large egg

90 g (3 oz) coconut sugar

90 g (3 oz) almond flour

½ tsp vanilla extract

6 tbsp chocolate chips

pinch of salt

METHOD

- Preheat the oven to 190°C (375°F) and line a baking sheet with parchment paper.
- In a bowl, mix the Greek yogurt, egg, sugar, vanilla extract, and salt until smooth.
- Gradually add almond flour and mix until a cookie dough forms. If it is too sticky, add a little extra flour; if too dry, add more yogurt.
- Fold in chocolate chips.
- Scoop out 9 equal portions of dough, shape into cookies, and place on the baking sheet, leaving space between them.
- Bake for 10–12 minutes until the edges turn light golden brown.
- Let cool completely before serving.

Note: 1 serving is 1 cookie.

ENERGY 181 Cal	CARBS 19 g	PROTEIN 6 g	FAT 9 g

WEEK 6 MEAL PLAN

DAY	BREAKFAST	LUNCH	SNACK	DINNER
Monday	Zucchini Breakfast Pizza Crust	Sweet Potato Cottage Pie	Lemon Chia Energy Balls	Baked Greek Meatballs with Tzatziki
Tuesday	Zucchini Breakfast Pizza Crust	Sweet Potato Cottage Pie	5-Ingredient Orange Cake	Baked Greek Meatballs with Tzatziki
Wednesday	Potato Cheese Omelet	capsicum Beef Tacos	5-Ingredient Orange Cake	Harissa Cod with Creamy White Beans
Thursday	Potato Cheese Omelet	capsicum Beef Tacos	Lemon Chia Energy Balls	Salmon Quinoa Bowl
Friday	PBK Breakfast Parfait	Beef Shawarma Wraps	Orange Turmeric Smoothie	Salmon Quinoa Bowl
Saturday	PBK Breakfast Parfait	Vietnamese Chicken Noodle Salad	Orange Turmeric Smoothie	Meal Out – Enjoy!
Sunday	Orange Turmeric Smoothie	Vietnamese Chicken Noodle Salad	Lemon Chia Energy Balls	Beef Shawarma Wraps

SHOPPING LIST

Produce

6 red onions
3 brown onions
garlic
parsley
dill
mint
280 g (10 oz) zucchini (courgette)
3 cucumbers
4 carrots
907 g (2 lbs) sweet potatoes
3 oranges
2 lemons
1 red chilli
4 red capsicums
200 g (7 oz) cherry tomatoes

Protein

Greek yogurt
mozzarella cheese
Cheddar cheese
Parmesan cheese (Parmigiano Reggiano)
1 tbsp all-natural peanut butter (crunchy)
lean ground beef
ground turkey breast (extra lean)
cooked chicken breast
flank steak
salmon fillets
10 eggs
cod fillets (white fish)
Whole milk

Dry Goods

all-purpose flour
orzo
vermicelli rice noodles
quinoa (uncooked)
unsweetened coconut flakes
sunflower seeds
pumpkin seeds
chia seeds
cashews
almonds
unsweetened desiccated coconut
almond flour
baking powder
cornstarch
salted peanuts
coconut sugar
ground turmeric
ground cinnamon
chilli flakes
ground flax seed
thyme
shawarma seasoning
dried oregano
dried basil
garlic powder
onion powder
taco seasoning

Staples & Misc

coconut oil
rice vinegar
Worcestershire sauce
fish sauce
honey
maple syrup
peanut butter
Dijon mustard
mayonnaise
vanilla extract
beef stock
canned cannellini beans

SERVES 2 | PREPARATION TIME: 15 MINUTES

POTATO CHEESE OMELET

INGREDIENTS

1 red onion, peeled and sliced

340 g potatoes, thinly sliced

6 large eggs

4 g fresh parsley, chopped (reserve a few leaves for garnish)

90 g (3 oz) mozzarella, shredded

¼ tsp chilli flakes

½ tsp garlic powder

salt and black pepper, to taste

METHOD

- Heat 1 tbsp olive oil in a pan over medium heat. Add the onion and cook for 3–4 minutes until soft. Remove and set aside.
- In the same pan, cook the potatoes for about 3 minutes per side until golden. Season with salt and black pepper.
- In a bowl, whisk the eggs and season them with salt. Stir in the cooked onion, parsley, garlic powder, chilli flakes, salt, and black pepper. Pour the egg mixture over the potatoes. Cover and cook over low heat for 3 minutes.
- Carefully flip the omelet. Sprinkle with mozzarella, cover, and cook for 2 more minutes until the cheese melts. Fold in half.
- Garnish with parsley and serve.

ENERGY **504** Cal | CARBS **33** g | PROTEIN **30** g | FAT **28** g

SERVES 14 | PREPARATION TIME: 15 MINUTES

STOVE TOP TURMERIC GRANOLA

INGREDIENTS

1 tbsp coconut oil

160 g unsweetened coconut flakes

4 tbsp sunflower seeds

4 tbsp pumpkin seeds

2 tbsp chia seeds

90 g (3 oz) cashews

90 g (3 oz) almonds

1 tsp ground turmeric

1 tsp ground cinnamon

1 tsp vanilla extract

3 tbsp maple syrup

METHOD

- In a bowl, combine coconut flakes, seeds, nuts, turmeric, and cinnamon.
- Heat the coconut oil in a non-stick skillet over medium-low heat. Add the dry mix and toast for 5 minutes, stirring constantly.
- Stir in the vanilla extract and maple syrup. Cook for 3–4 minutes more until golden and sticky.
- Spread onto a parchment-lined baking sheet and let cool into clusters. Store in an airtight container at room temperature for up to 2–3 weeks.

Note: Makes ~3½ cups; 1 serving = ~¼ cup.

ENERGY **213** Cal | CARBS **11** g | PROTEIN **17** g | FAT **4** g

SERVES 6 | PREPARATION TIME: 45 MINUTES

ZUCCHINI BREAKFAST PIZZA CRUST

INGREDIENTS

280 g (10 oz) shredded or spiralized zucchini

60 g (2 oz) shredded mozzarella cheese

60 g (2 oz) all-purpose flour

1 clove garlic, minced

1 tsp dried oregano

1 tsp dried basil

1 egg, beaten

salt, to taste

METHOD

- Preheat the oven to 290°C (550°F) on a broil. Toss zucchini with 1 tsp salt and let sit for 15 minutes. Squeeze out moisture using a clean towel.
- Add cheese, flour, garlic, herbs, egg, and ½ tsp salt to the zucchini. Mix well.
- Spread the mixture into a 13 cm (5-inch) circle, about 6mm (¼-inch) thick, on a baking sheet lined with parchment. Lightly score the edges.
- Bake for 8–10 minutes until starting to brown.
- Reduce the oven to 200°C (400°F). Top with your favourite toppings and bake for another 8–12 minutes.
- Garnish with fresh herbs and serve.

Suggested Toppings (optional):

pizza sauce

asparagus stalks, halved and cut into 2-inch pieces

cherry tomatoes, sliced

drizzle olive oil

eggs

Parmesan cheese

fresh basil or herbs

Note: Suggested toppings are not included in nutritional breakdown.

ENERGY **75** Cal	CARBS **8** g	PROTEIN **4** g	FAT **3** g

SERVES 3 | PREPARATION TIME: 15 MINUTES

PBJ BREAKFAST PARFAIT

INGREDIENTS

450 g (16 oz) Greek yogurt

3 tbsp crunchy peanut butter

3 tbsp Easy Berry Chia Jam

1 serving of Stove Top Turmeric Granola, to serve

Easy Berry Chia Jam:

375 g (13 oz) frozen blueberries

2 tbsp chia seeds

1 tbsp orange juice

2 tbsp honey

METHOD

- Combine blueberries, chia seeds, and orange juice in a bowl. Stir and let sit at room temperature for 1–2 hours or refrigerate overnight.
- Mash slightly, then stir in honey and let sit for another 20–30 minutes to thicken.
- For each parfait, layer the yogurt, followed by peanut butter and chia jam. Repeat.
- Refrigerate until serving.
- Top with **Stove Top Turmeric Granola** (see page 183) just before serving.

ENERGY **325** Cal | CARBS **23** g | PROTEIN **20** g | FAT **17** g

SERVES 6 | PREPARATION TIME: 1 HOUR 5 MINUTES

SWEET POTATO COTTAGE PIE

INGREDIENTS

900 g sweet potatoes, peeled and chopped

125 g (4 oz) Greek yogurt

2 tbsp unsalted butter

2 tsp cornstarch

240 ml (1 cup) beef stock

450 g lean ground beef

2 medium carrots, thinly sliced

1 medium brown onion, chopped

3 cloves garlic, minced

2 tbsp tomato paste

2 tsp thyme

170 g (6 oz) frozen peas

1 tbsp Worcestershire sauce

salt and black pepper, to taste

METHOD

- Preheat the oven to 220°C (425°F).
- Boil sweet potatoes until tender (10–12 minutes). Drain, return to pot, and cook for 3 minutes over low heat to dry. Mash with yogurt, butter, and ¼ tsp salt. Set aside.
- Whisk cornstarch into stock and set aside.
- In an oven-safe skillet over medium-high heat, brown the beef for about 7 minutes.
- Add carrots, onion, and garlic; cook 6 minutes more.
- Stir in tomato paste and thyme. Cook for 1 minute.
- Add stock mixture, peas, Worcestershire sauce, ¾ tsp pepper, and ¼ tsp salt. Stir and simmer for 3 minutes until thickened.
- Spread sweet potato mash evenly on top.
- Bake for 15–20 minutes until heated through and lightly browned. Garnish with fresh chives (optional) and serve.

ENERGY **369** Cal | CARBS **42** g | PROTEIN **21** g | FAT **13** g

STAUB

SERVES 6 | PREPARATION TIME: 25 MINUTES

CAPSICUM BEEF NACHOS

INGREDIENTS

4 red capsicums (red bell peppers), cut into chunks

450 g (1 lb) ground beef

1 brown onion, diced

3 tbsp taco seasoning

230 g (8 oz) Cheddar cheese, grated

salt and black pepper to taste.

METHOD

- Preheat the oven to 220°C (425°F).
- Line a baking tray with parchment.
- Place capsicum (bell pepper) chunks on the tray.
- Season with salt and black pepper. Bake for 10 minutes.
- Heat a dry pan over medium heat. Add ground beef and break it up as it cooks.
- Add the onion and taco seasoning. Cook for 10 minutes until browned.
- Spread cooked beef and onion over the baked capsicums (bell peppers).
- Top with cheese.
- Return to the oven for 10 more minutes.

Serving suggestions (optional): chopped coriander (cilantro), salsa, guacamole, lime wedges.

ENERGY **337** Cal	CARBS **12** g	PROTEIN **25** g	FAT **21** g

SERVES 4 | PREPARATION TIME: 13 MINUTES

VIETNAMESE CHICKEN NOODLE SALAD

INGREDIENTS

Nuoc Cham Dressing:

1 tbsp lime juice

2 tbsp coconut sugar

2 tbsp fish sauce

2 tbsp rice vinegar

1 red bird's eye chilli (red chilli pepper), deseeded and diced

2 cloves garlic, minced

Salad:

400 g (14 oz) cooked chicken breasts, shredded

125 g (4 oz) vermicelli rice noodles

½ cucumber, peeled and cut into ribbons

1 large carrot, shredded

8 g fresh coriander (cilantro), chopped

8 fresh mint leaves, sliced

30 g (1 oz) salted peanuts, chopped

METHOD

- In a small bowl, combine all dressing ingredients and set aside.
- Place rice noodles in a large pot.
- Cover with boiling water and let sit for 3 minutes.
- Drain and rinse under cold water.
- In a large bowl, mix the noodles with cucumber, carrot, coriander (cilantro), mint, chicken, and peanuts.
- Pour over the dressing and toss to combine.
- Top with extra herbs and peanuts if desired.
- Serve immediately.

ENERGY **339** Cal | CARBS **35** g | PROTEIN **34** g | FAT **7** g

SERVES 2 | PREPARATION TIME: 25 MINUTES

HARISSA COD WITH CREAMY WHITE BEANS

INGREDIENTS

30 g (1 oz) harissa paste

60 g (2 oz) breadcrumbs

300 g (10 oz) cod fillets

400 g (14 oz) can cannellini beans

50 ml (1.7 fl. oz) whole milk

30 g (1 oz) fresh parsley, chopped

½ lemon, juiced

30 g (1 oz) Parmesan cheese, grated

1 tsp chilli flakes

1 clove garlic, peeled

1 tbsp olive oil

salt and black pepper to taste

METHOD

- Preheat the oven to 200°C (390°F).
- Mix harissa paste, olive oil, and breadcrumbs into a spreadable paste.
- Spread over the cod fillets and bake for 12–15 minutes.
- Add beans (with liquid), garlic, milk, and 50 ml (1.7 fl. oz) water to a pot.
- Simmer for 10–15 minutes until thickened.
- Remove and discard the garlic.
- Stir in parsley, Parmesan cheese, and lemon juice.
- Season with salt and black pepper.
- Serve the cod over the creamy beans.
- Garnish with chilli flakes, extra cheese, and parsley if desired.

ENERGY **427** Cal | CARBS **42** g | PROTEIN **31** g | FAT **15** g

SERVES 4 | PREPARATION TIME: 25 MINUTES

SALMON QUINOA BOWL

INGREDIENTS

Bowls:

180 g (6 oz) quinoa (raw)
450 g (1 lb) salmon fillets, cut into bite-size pieces
1 tbsp honey
½ lemon, juiced
1 tbsp paprika
½ tsp garlic powder
½ tsp onion powder
2 tbsp olive oil
½ tsp salt

Cucumber Salad:

1 cucumber, diced
7 g fresh dill, chopped
½ lemon, juiced
2 tbsp olive oil
salt and black pepper to taste

Sauce:

60 g (2 oz) mayonnaise
1 tsp Dijon mustard
½ lemon, juiced
¼ tsp dill, chopped
salt and black pepper to taste

METHOD

- Preheat the oven to 230°C (450°F).
- Cook quinoa according to package instructions, then drain and fluff.
- In a bowl, mix olive oil, honey, lemon juice, paprika, garlic powder, onion powder, and salt.
- Toss in salmon to coat.
- Spread salmon on a baking sheet and bake for 10–12 minutes.
- For the cucumber salad, mix diced cucumber with dill, olive oil, and lemon juice.
- Season with salt and black pepper to taste.
- For the sauce, whisk together mayonnaise, mustard, lemon juice, dill, salt, and black pepper.
- To serve, divide quinoa between bowls.
- Top with salmon, cucumber salad, and a drizzle of the sauce.

ENERGY **573** Cal | CARBS **37** g | PROTEIN **32** g | FAT **33** g

SERVES 4 | PREPARATION TIME: 30 MINUTES

BAKED GREEK MEATBALLS WITH TZATZIKI

INGREDIENTS

Meatballs:

450 g (1 lb) ground turkey breast

1 egg

60 g (2 oz) breadcrumbs

½ red onion, minced

2 cloves garlic, minced

2 tbsp fresh mint, finely chopped

½ tsp dried oregano

1 tsp salt

black pepper to taste

Bowls:

300 g (11 oz) dry orzo

140 g (5 oz) cherry tomatoes, halved

¼ cucumber, diced

¼ red onion, sliced

2 tbsp olive oil

fresh mint, to serve

4 servings Homemade Tzatziki Sauce

METHOD

- Preheat the oven to 175°C (350°F).
- Line a baking sheet with parchment.
- Mix all meatball ingredients together.
- Form into 2-tbsp-sized balls (16 meatballs).
- Bake for 14–16 minutes until fully cooked.
- Cook orzo according to package instructions.
- Drain and toss with olive oil.
- In a bowl, combine cherry tomatoes, cucumber, and red onion.
- Season with salt and black pepper.
- Assemble bowls with orzo, salad, meatballs, and tzatziki.
- Garnish with mint.

ENERGY **633** Cal | CARBS **72** g | PROTEIN **39** g | FAT **21** g

SERVES 4 | PREPARATION TIME: 30 MINUTES

BEEF SHAWARMA WRAPS

INGREDIENTS

Beef Shawarma:

450 g (1 lb) flank steak, thinly sliced

½ lemon, juiced

4 cloves garlic, minced or grated

3 tsp shawarma seasoning

3 tbsp olive oil

1 tbsp white vinegar

salt and black pepper to taste

1 tbsp olive oil (for cooking)

METHOD

- In a bowl, mix olive oil, lemon juice, white vinegar, garlic, seasoning, salt, and black pepper.
- Toss the beef in the marinade.
- Let sit for 10 minutes.
- Heat olive oil in a skillet over medium-high.
- Cook beef in batches, 1–2 minutes per side, until browned.
- Serve wrapped in pita with desired toppings.

Suggested serving (optional, not included in nutrition information): pitas, sliced tomatoes, shredded cucumber, sliced red onion, rocket (arugula), pickles, Homemade Tzatziki Sauce.

ENERGY **307** Cal | CARBS **1** g | PROTEIN **24** g | FAT **23** g

SERVES 6 | PREPARATION TIME: 5 MINUTES

HOMEMADE TZATZIKI SAUCE

INGREDIENTS

60 g (2.1 oz) cucumber, grated
250 g (9 oz) Greek yogurt
1 tbsp lemon juice
1 clove garlic, grated
1 tbsp fresh dill, chopped
1 tbsp fresh mint, chopped
½ tbsp olive oil
¼ tsp salt

METHOD

- Squeeze excess water from the cucumber using a towel.
- Combine all ingredients in a bowl.
- Stir well.
- Chill until ready to serve.

ENERGY **46** Cal | CARBS **3** g | PROTEIN **4** g | FAT **2** g

SERVES 12 | PREPARATION TIME: 1 HOUR 35 MINUTES

5-INGREDIENT ORANGE CAKE

INGREDIENTS

2 whole oranges

3 eggs

230 g (8 oz) honey

300 g (10 oz) almond flour

2 tsp baking powder

METHOD

- Place oranges in a pot, cover with water, and bring to a boil.
- Simmer for 25 minutes.
- Drain and cool.
- Preheat the oven to 160°C (325°F).
- Line or grease a 25 cm (10-inch) cake pan.
- In a bowl, whisk eggs and honey.
- Add almond flour and baking powder.
- Roughly chop the boiled oranges (remove seeds but keep peel).
- Blend until smooth.
- Stir into batter.
- Pour into the pan and bake for 55–65 minutes or until a toothpick comes out clean.
- Cool 10 minutes before serving.

ENERGY **241** Cal | CARBS **24** g | PROTEIN **7** g | FAT **13** g

MAKES 12 BALLS | PREPARATION TIME: 15 MINUTES

LEMON CHIA ENERGY BALLS

INGREDIENTS

150 g (5 oz) cashews

125 g (4 oz) shredded coconut

3 tbsp maple syrup

60 ml (2 fl. oz) lemon juice

2 tbsp lemon zest

2 tbsp chia seeds

To coat:

30 g (1 oz) unsweetened desiccated coconut

METHOD

- In a food processor, blend cashews and shredded coconut into a coarse meal.
- Add maple syrup, lemon juice, and zest.
- Blend until a sticky dough forms.
- Add chia seeds and pulse to mix.
- Adjust texture with more coconut or water as needed.
- Roll dough into 1-tbsp-sized balls and coat in desiccated coconut.
- Chill on parchment.
- Store in the fridge for up to 1 week.

Note: 1 energy ball is 1 serving.

ENERGY **216** Cal | CARBS **14** g | PROTEIN **4** g | FAT **16** g

SERVES 1 | PREPARATION TIME: 5 MINUTES

ORANGE TURMERIC SMOOTHIE

INGREDIENTS

1 orange, peeled

1 carrot, peeled and chopped

115 g (4 oz) Greek yogurt

1 tsp ground flax seeds

¼ tsp ground turmeric

METHOD

- Add all ingredients to a high-speed blender.
- Blitz until smooth.
- Serve immediately.

ENERGY **216** Cal | CARBS **31** g | PROTEIN **14** g | FAT **4** g

WEEK 7 MEAL PLAN

DAY	BREAKFAST	LUNCH	SNACK	DINNER
Monday	Overnight Blueberry Chia Protein Oats	Spinach & Feta-Stuffed Chicken Breasts	Spinach Feta Almond Biscuits	Parchment Garlic Butter Haddock
Tuesday	Spinach & Feta Tortilla	Spinach & Feta-Stuffed Chicken Breasts	Spinach Feta Almond Biscuits	Salmon Bites with Maple Tahini Dressing
Wednesday	Spinach & Feta Tortilla	Salmon Bites with Maple Tahini Dressing	Soft Banana Oat Cookies	Chicken Kale Salad with Maple Tahini Dressing
Thursday	Sausage & Potato Breakfast Hash	Chicken Kale Salad with Maple Tahini Dressing	Soft Banana Oat Cookies	Chicken Kale Salad with Maple Tahini Dressing
Friday	Sausage & Potato Breakfast Hash	Chicken Kale Salad with Maple Tahini Dressing	PB Coffee Protein Smoothie	Spiced Tomato-Baked Chicken Thighs
Saturday	Tomato, White Bean & Egg Skillet	rocket, Strawberry & Avo Steak Salad	Soft Banana Oat Cookies	Meal Out – Enjoy!
Sunday	Overnight Blueberry Chia Protein Oats	rocket, Strawberry & Avo Steak Salad	PB Coffee Protein Smoothie	Spiced Tomato-Baked Chicken Thighs

SHOPPING LIST

Produce

5 bananas
500 g (1.1 lbs) spinach
200 g (7 oz) strawberries
2 avocados
2 zucchinis (courgettes)
220 g (7.5 oz) carrots
3 tomatoes
284 g (10 oz) cherry tomatoes
4 brown onions
garlic
sun-dried tomatoes
green onions (scallions)
parsley
blueberries
1 lemon
ginger
frozen peas

Protein

10 eggs
chicken breast
herby chicken sausages
chicken thighs, skinless
salmon, skinless
cottage cheese
shredded cheese
feta cheese
vanilla protein powder
Parmesan cheese, grated

Dry Goods

209 g (7.4 oz) oats
128 g (4.5 oz) oat flour
113 g (4 oz) almond flour
dried cranberries
pumpkin seeds
pecans
walnuts
pine nuts
sliced almonds
raisins
chia seeds
ground flaxseed
baking powder
baking soda
basmati rice
dark chocolate chips
coconut sugar
2 flour tortillas
garlic powder
onion powder
Italian seasoning
dried oregano
smoked paprika
paprika
chilli flakes
cumin
ground turmeric
ground cinnamon
ground coriander

Staples & Misc

425 g (15 oz) cannellini beans
peanut butter
80 g (2.8 oz) tomato paste
coconut oil
tahini
maple syrup
rice vinegar
oat milk
unsweetened almond milk
brewed coffee
tamari
vanilla extract

SERVES 2 | PREPARATION TIME: 5 MINUTES

OVERNIGHT BLUEBERRY CHIA PROTEIN OATS

INGREDIENTS

90 g (3 oz) oats

1 tbsp chia seeds

300 ml (10 fl. oz) oat milk

3 tbsp vanilla protein powder

2 tsp ground flaxseed

150 g (5 oz) blueberries

1 tbsp natural peanut butter

2 tbsp pecans, chopped

METHOD

- Combine oats, chia seeds, and oat milk in a bowl.
- Stir and refrigerate for 8 hours or overnight.
- Stir in protein powder and flaxseed.
- Add more oat milk, one tablespoon at a time, if too thick.
- Divide into bowls and top with blueberries, peanut butter, and pecans.

ENERGY **457** Cal | CARBS **55** g | PROTEIN **21** g | FAT **17** g

SERVES 2 | PREPARATION TIME: 35 MINUTES

SPINACH & FETA TORTILLA

INGREDIENTS

4 large eggs

125 g (4 oz) cottage cheese

60 g (2 oz) shredded cheese

30 g (1 oz) crumbled feta cheese

30 g (1 oz) sun-dried tomatoes, drained and chopped

30 g (1 oz) spinach, packed and chopped

2 flour tortillas

½ tsp garlic powder

¼ tsp Italian seasoning

¼ tsp salt

fresh basil, to garnish

METHOD

- Preheat the oven to 175°C (350°F).
- Blend eggs, cottage cheese, and shredded cheese until smooth.
- Stir in spinach, sun-dried tomatoes, feta cheese, spices, and salt.
- Grease a 23–25 cm (9–10 inch) pie dish and layer tortillas inside.
- Pour in the filling and spread evenly.
- Bake for 20–25 minutes until set.
- Garnish with basil and serve.

ENERGY **454** Cal | CARBS **24** g | PROTEIN **31** g | FAT **26** g

SERVES 3 | PREPARATION TIME: 30 MINUTES

TOMATO, WHITE BEAN & EGG SKILLET

INGREDIENTS

3 slices bread, chopped

4 tbsp Parmesan cheese, grated

2 cloves garlic, minced

280 g (10 oz) cherry tomatoes

400 g (14 oz) can cannellini beans, drained

½ tsp dried oregano

6 eggs

fresh basil, to serve

salt and black pepper to taste

2 tbsp olive oil

METHOD

- Heat 1 tbsp olive oil in a large skillet over medium-high heat.
- Add bread and fry until golden.
- Toss toasted bread with Parmesan in a bowl.
- Wipe the skillet clean, add remaining olive oil, and cook garlic for 30–60 seconds.
- Add tomatoes and beans.
- Cook for 7–10 minutes until tomatoes burst.
- Stir in most of the bread.
- Make 4 wells and crack in eggs.
- Cover and cook for 3–4 minutes.
- To serve, top with remaining bread, season with salt and black pepper, and garnish with basil.

ENERGY **428** Cal | CARBS **31** g | PROTEIN **22** g | FAT **24** g

SERVES 2 | PREPARATION TIME: 25 MINUTES

SAUSAGE & POTATO BREAKFAST HASH

INGREDIENTS

1 tbsp butter

340 g (12 oz) herby chicken sausages, skinned

1 onion, sliced

100 g (3.5 oz) potatoes (skin on), grated, moisture squeezed out

2 eggs

salt and black pepper to taste

METHOD

- Heat butter in a pan on medium heat.
- Add sausages and brown the meat.
- Add onion and cook until soft.
- Set mixture aside.
- Add grated potatoes and cook until golden.
- Set aside.
- Crack in eggs and cook until whites are set.
- Divide everything between two plates, season with salt and black pepper, and serve.

ENERGY 359 Cal	CARBS 18 g	PROTEIN 38 g	FAT 15 g

SERVES 4 | PREPARATION TIME: 25 MINUTES

ROCKET (ARUGULA), STRAWBERRY & AVO STEAK SALAD

INGREDIENTS

600 g (1.3 lb) ribeye steaks, boneless

170 g (6 oz) rocket (arugula)

200 g (7 oz) strawberries, quartered

2 avocados, sliced

6 servings Maple Tahini Dressing

½ tsp olive oil

salt and black pepper to taste

METHOD

- Season steak with salt, black pepper, and olive oil.
- Sear steaks 4–7 minutes per side.
- Rest for 5–10 minutes, then slice.
- Toss rocket (arugula) with Maple Tahini Dressing, then divide onto plates.
- Top with strawberries, avocado, and steak.
- Drizzle with remaining dressing.

ENERGY **596** Cal | CARBS **23** g | PROTEIN **36** g | FAT **40** g

SERVES 2 | PREPARATION TIME: 35 MINUTES

SPINACH & FETA-STUFFED CHICKEN BREASTS

INGREDIENTS

1 clove garlic, chopped

90 g (3 oz) spinach

40 g (1.5 oz) feta cheese, diced

20 g (0.7 oz) sun-dried tomatoes, chopped

300 g (10 oz) chicken breasts (2 small)

1 tsp paprika

1 tsp chilli flakes

2 tbsp olive oil

salt and black pepper to taste

METHOD

- Heat 1 tbsp olive oil in a pan.
- Sauté garlic for 2 minutes.
- Add spinach and cook until wilted.
- Season with salt and black pepper.
- Mix in feta cheese and sun-dried tomatoes.
- Set aside.
- Butterfly the chicken breasts and gently pound to flatten.
- Season with paprika, chilli flakes, salt, and black pepper.
- Add filling, fold, and secure with toothpicks.
- Heat remaining olive oil and cook chicken for 20 minutes, turning to brown all sides.
- Serve with salad.

ENERGY **336** Cal | CARBS **9** g | PROTEIN **39** g | FAT **16** g

SERVES 4 | PREPARATION TIME: 25 MINUTES

SALMON BITES WITH MAPLE TAHINI DRESSING

INGREDIENTS

680 g (1.5 lb) salmon, skinless, cut into cubes

1 tsp garlic powder

1 tsp onion powder

2 tbsp olive oil

½ tsp salt

½ tsp ground black pepper

4 tbsp Maple Tahini Dressing

4 tbsp green onions, sliced, for garnish

2 tsp sesame seeds, for garnish

METHOD

- Toss salmon with olive oil, spices, salt, and black pepper.
- Heat a skillet over medium heat.
- Cook salmon for 8–10 minutes, turning to brown on all sides.
- To serve, drizzle **Maple Tahini Dressing** (see page 232) over cooked salmon.
- Garnish with green onions and sesame seeds.

Serving suggestion: Over rice or quinoa.

ENERGY 364 Cal	CARBS 6 g	PROTEIN 40 g	FAT 20 g

SERVES 4 | PREPARATION TIME: 25 MINUTES

CHICKEN KALE SALAD WITH MAPLE TAHINI DRESSING

INGREDIENTS

juice of 1 lemon

2 cloves garlic, crushed

680 g (1.5 lb) chicken breast

1 tsp paprika

½ tsp cumin

2 tbsp olive oil

1 tsp olive oil (for cooking)

6 tbsp Maple Tahini Dressing, divided

284 g (10 oz) kale leaves

1 avocado, cubed

30 g (1 oz) dried cranberries

30 g (1 oz) pumpkin seeds

½ tsp salt

½ tsp ground black pepper

METHOD

- Mix olive oil, lemon juice, and garlic in a bowl.
- Add chicken and coat with spices, salt, and black pepper.
- Let it marinate.
- Mix **Maple Tahini Dressing** (see page 232) into kale.
- Heat olive oil in a pan over medium heat and cook chicken for 5–7 minutes per side or until cooked through.
- Let rest, then slice.
- Top salad with avocado, cranberries, pumpkin seeds, and chicken.
- Drizzle with remaining dressing.

ENERGY 546 Cal	CARBS 22 g	PROTEIN 47 g	FAT 30 g

SERVES 2 | PREPARATION TIME: 25 MINUTES

PARCHMENT GARLIC BUTTER HADDOCK

INGREDIENTS

1½ tbsp soft butter

1 tbsp parsley, chopped

1 clove garlic, minced

2 small zucchinis, sliced

1 medium carrot, sliced

300 g (10 oz) haddock

salt and black pepper to taste

METHOD

- Preheat the oven to 205°C (400°F).
- Cut two 45 cm (18 inch) parchment sheets and fold in half.
- Mix butter, parsley, and garlic.
- Divide vegetables onto parchment.
- Season fish with salt and black pepper.
- Place on top and spread with butter mix.
- Fold and crimp parchment to seal.
- Bake for 15–16 minutes until the fish is cooked.
- Open and serve.

Tip: If you can't find haddock, basa fillets or flathead work just as well.

ENERGY **290** Cal | CARBS **10** g | PROTEIN **40** g | FAT **10** g

STAUB

SERVES 8 | PREPARATION TIME: 1 HOUR

SPICED TOMATO-BAKED CHICKEN THIGHS

INGREDIENTS

For the Chicken:

800 g (1.8 lb) skinless chicken thighs

3 medium brown onions, thinly sliced

3 tomatoes, sliced

fresh parsley, to garnish

salt and black pepper to taste

For the Spiced Rub:

80 g (2.8 oz) tomato paste

juice of 1 lemon

4 cloves garlic, minced

1 tsp dried oregano

1 tsp smoked paprika

1 tsp ground cumin

80 ml (2.8 fl. oz) olive oil

1 tsp ground black pepper

METHOD

- Preheat the oven to 220°C (425°F).
- Season chicken with salt and black pepper.
- Mix the spiced rub ingredients with olive oil and black pepper.
- Coat chicken thoroughly.
- Brush a baking dish with olive oil, layer three-quarters of the onions, and place chicken on top.
- Add tomatoes and remaining onions.
- Pour water into corners without disturbing the rub.
- Bake for 40 minutes.
- Grill chicken for 1–3 minutes to crisp.
- Rest 5–10 minutes, garnish with parsley, and serve.

Serving suggestion: Serve with **Spiced Veggie Pilaf Rice** (see page 235).

ENERGY **174** Cal | CARBS **9** g | PROTEIN **21** g | FAT **6** g

SERVES 24 TBSP | PREPARATION TIME: 5 MINUTES

MAPLE TAHINI DRESSING

INGREDIENTS

180 g (6 oz) tahini
80 ml (2.7 fl. oz) maple syrup
80 ml (2.7 fl. oz) tamari
4 tsp rice vinegar
4 tsp ginger, grated
4 cloves garlic, crushed
salt to taste

METHOD

- Whisk all ingredients together until smooth.
- Add 1 tsp water to start, then add 2–7 tsp more if needed for a thick, pourable consistency.
- Season with salt.

ENERGY **60** Cal | CARBS **4** g | PROTEIN **2** g | FAT **4** g

SERVES 8 | PREPARATION TIME: 30 MINUTES

SPICED VEGGIE PILAF RICE

INGREDIENTS

400 g (14 oz) basmati rice

1 small brown onion, finely chopped

2 cloves garlic, minced

135 g (5 oz) frozen peas

150 g (5 oz) carrots, chopped

½ tsp coriander

½ tsp paprika

¼ tsp ground turmeric

2 tbsp olive oil

18.2 fl. oz (540 ml) water

salt and black pepper to taste

METHOD

- Rinse rice several times until water is clear.
- Soak for 10 minutes.
- In a large pan, heat olive oil.
- Sauté onion and garlic for 3–5 minutes.
- Add peas and carrots.
- Season with salt, black pepper, and spices.
- Cook for 5 minutes until carrots soften.
- Drain rice, add to pan, and stir to coat.
- Pour in water, season with more salt, and bring to a boil.
- Cover and simmer on low for 15–20 minutes until liquid is absorbed.
- Let it rest 5–10 minutes before serving.

Serving suggestion: Serve with Spiced Tomato-Baked Chicken Thighs.

Optional Nut Toppings: walnut halves (toasted), pine nuts (toasted), sliced almonds (toasted).

ENERGY 240 Cal	CARBS 46 g	PROTEIN 5 g	FAT 4 g

MAKES 6 | PREPARATION TIME: 40 MINUTES

SPINACH FETA ALMOND BISCUITS

INGREDIENTS

30 g (1 oz) green onions, chopped

140 g (5 oz) fresh spinach, chopped

4–5 egg whites

100 g (3.5 oz) almond flour

1 tsp baking powder

100 g (3.5 oz) crumbled feta cheese

1 tbsp olive oil

salt and black pepper to taste

METHOD

- Preheat the oven to 175°C (350°F).
- Line a baking sheet with parchment.
- Heat olive oil in a pan and cook green onions for 1–2 minutes.
- Add spinach and cook until wilted.
- Season with salt and black pepper.
- Cool slightly.
- Mix spinach mixture with egg whites, almond flour, baking powder, and feta cheese.
- Form 6 biscuits or drop spoonfuls onto the baking sheet.
- Bake for 20–25 minutes until the edges are golden.
- Cool slightly before serving.

Note: 1 biscuit is 1 serving.

ENERGY 204 Cal	CARBS 6 g	PROTEIN 9 g	FAT 16 g

MAKES 20 | PREPARATION TIME: 25 MINUTES

SOFT BANANA OAT COOKIES

INGREDIENTS

125 g (4 oz) rolled oats

125 g (4 oz) oat flour

200 g (7 oz) bananas, mashed (about 2 bananas)

12 g (0.4 oz) coconut oil, softened

2 large eggs

100 g (3.5 oz) coconut sugar

1 tsp vanilla extract

½ tsp cinnamon

½ tsp baking soda

80 g (2.8 oz) dark chocolate chips

¼ tsp salt

METHOD

- Preheat the oven to 175°C (350°F).
- In a bowl, whisk bananas, eggs, sugar, coconut oil, and vanilla extract until smooth.
- Stir in oats, oat flour, cinnamon, baking soda, and salt.
- Fold in chocolate chips.
- Scoop 2-tbsp-sized portions onto a lined baking sheet, 2.5 cm (1 inch) apart.
- Bake for 12–15 minutes until edges are browned.
- Cool and store airtight.

Note: 1 cookie is 1 serving.

ENERGY **127** Cal | CARBS **14** g | PROTEIN **2** g | FAT **7** g

SERVES 2 | PREPARATION TIME: 5 MINUTES

PB COFFEE PROTEIN SMOOTHIE

INGREDIENTS

400 ml (13.5 fl. oz) coffee, cooled

30 g (1 oz) peanut butter

180 g (6 oz) ripe banana, frozen (about 1½ bananas)

60 g (2 oz) protein powder (vanilla or chocolate)

2–3 tbsp almond milk, unsweetened, as needed

METHOD

- Add coffee, peanut butter, banana, and protein powder to a blender.
- Blend until smooth and creamy.
- Adjust with a splash of almond milk for desired consistency.
- Serve immediately.

ENERGY 305 Cal	CARBS 28 g	PROTEIN 28 g	FAT 9 g

INDEX

First published in 2026 by New Holland Publishers

newhollandpublishers.com

Copyright © 2026 New Holland Publishers
Copyright © 2026 in text: Faye James
Copyright © 2026 in images: Darrin James

All rights reserved. No part of this publication may be reproduced, stored in a retrieval system or transmitted, in any form or by any means, electronic, mechanical, photocopying, recording or otherwise, without the prior written permission of the publishers and copyright holders.

A record of this book is held at the National Library of Australia.

ISBN 9781742573533

Text: Faye James
Photography: Exceed
Recipe development: Faye James

Managing Director: Fiona Schultz
General Manager/Publisher: Olga Dementiev
Designer: Andrew Davies
Production Director: Arlene Gippert

Keep up with New Holland Publishers:

NewHollandPublishers
@newhollandpublishers

US $19.99

UK £14.99